Project-Based Learning

for Gifted Students

A Handbook for the
21st-Century Classroom

Project-Based Learning
for Gifted Students

A Handbook for the
21st-Century Classroom

TODD STANLEY

P R U F R O C K P R E S S I N C.
W A C O , T E X A S

Library of Congress Cataloging-in-Publication Data

Stanley, Todd.
 Project-based learning for gifted students : a handbook for the 21st-century classroom / by Todd Stanley.
    p. cm.
 Includes bibliographical references.
 ISBN 978-1-59363-830-6 (pbk.)
 1. Gifted children--Education--United States. 2. Project method in teaching. I. Title.

 LC3993.9.S727 2012
 371.95--dc23

                              2011031625

Edited by Sarah Morrison

Cover and layout design by Raquel Trevino

ISBN-13: 978-1-59363-830-6

At the time of this book's publication, all facts and figures cited are the most current available. All telephone numbers, addresses, and website URLs are accurate and active. All publications, organizations, websites, and other resources exist as described in the book, and all have been verified. The author and Prufrock Press Inc. make no warranty or guarantee concerning the information and materials given out by organizations or content found at websites, and we are not responsible for any changes that occur after this book's publication. If you find an error, please contact Prufrock Press Inc.

Prufrock Press Inc.
P.O. Box 8813
Waco, TX 76714-8813
Phone: (800) 998-2208
Fax: (800) 240-0333
http://www.prufrock.com

Table of Contents

Introduction

■ ■ ■ ■ ■ ■ ■ ■ ■ ■ ■ ■ ■

This book is designed to help a teacher turn his or her gifted classroom in a project-based learning environment. There are numerous advantages associated with shifting from traditional learning to project-based learning. For instance, project-based learning:

- allows for more creativity,
- is easily differentiable for students of varying ability levels,
- motivates underachieving gifted students, and
- creates a passion for learning.

Teachers often claim that they cannot incorporate project-based learning into their classrooms because they have to cover specific state and national learning standards. Teachers sometimes lament that they are bound to these learning standards, but these standards can instead be viewed as building blocks from which projects can be built—projects that foster student understanding, rather than rote memorization. When planned and implemented thoughtfully, project-based learning works alongside state and national standards and complements them. This book provides strategies for how to plan projects using state and national standards as guidelines, so that students approach core concepts with new depth and passion.

Chapters 1–3 of this book explain the rationale behind project-based learning. What advantages does project-based learning provide for your gifted classroom? Where, when, and how is project-based learning best implemented? The rest of the book looks at the practical applications of using project-based learning in the gifted classroom. Chapter 4 deals with finding the structure that works best for you. The structure of your project-based learning classroom—how you create and run projects in a way that best fits your teaching style, your students' knowledge and abilities, and your classroom and resources—is the key to project-based learning. Once you have decided on a structure that best matches your and your students' situation, everything else usually falls into place. Chapter 5 discusses how to vary this structure, once you have found it, to adapt to your classroom's needs. Chapter 6 explains how to implement the structure you have chosen, which is greatly simplified after you have already considered your situation and how you might vary the structure as you are implementing it.

Because rubrics are the backbone of the project-based learning classroom, Chapter 7 is devoted to the topic of rubrics, discussing how to train students to use rubrics as a tool for self-empowerment and deeper learning. Chapter 8 addresses the importance of the classroom's physical setup, which can go a long way in terms of making projects run smoothly. The role of the teacher in a project-based classroom is covered in Chapter 9. Whereas in a traditional classroom, the teacher imparts knowledge to a passive audience of learners, in a project-based classroom, the teacher acts as a coach, enabling students to excel and supervising them as they progress. The reproducibles in Appendix A, including rubrics and learning contracts, can be used as they are or adapted to fit your classroom. The lessons in Appendix B provide samples of projects that I have used in my own classroom, with students' work included. You may use these same projects, or perhaps they will provide you with ideas for your own classroom.

Once you commit to project-based learning, you and your students will find it difficult ever to return to the traditional ways of teaching and learning. Having made my own classroom a project-based classroom, I know that I wouldn't have it any other way.

1

What Is Project-Based Learning, and Why Should We Use It?

■ ■ ■ ■ ■ ■ ■ ■ ■ ■ ■ ■

INTRODUCTION

In this chapter, project-based learning will be defined, and the elements that comprise project-based learning will be discussed. In addition, the value of using project-based learning in the gifted classroom will be explored. There are many benefits of project-based learning, among which are student independence, student empowerment, and the teacher's ability to tailor projects to the deep and varied needs of gifted students.

WHAT IS PROJECT-BASED LEARNING?

Project-based learning (PBL) is exactly what its name implies: learning through the process of completing a project over a period of time. A more comprehensive definition is as follows:

> projects are complex tasks based on challenging questions or problems, that involve students in design, problem-solving, decision making, or investigative activities; give students the opportunity to work relatively autonomously over extended periods of time; and culminate in realistic products or presentations. (Jones, Rasmussen, & Moffitt, 1997)

This style of teaching and learning is different from more traditional styles, such as teacher-led lectures or reading chapters in a textbook. In the latter methods, the student is *given* the information or skills being taught. The major difference in PBL is that students *discover* for themselves the process of learning. They are provided with the structure, resources, and guidance, but it is their responsibility to figure out how best to learn the material.

But what does PBL actually look like? In one project, students may be given 2 weeks to create presentations regarding the study of cells. The only parameters are that the topic must involve cells and that the product (a presentation) must include a visual aid. Students must determine for themselves how their time should be spent over the course of 2 weeks: They may allocate their time to conducting research, creating the presentation, producing the visual aid, or practicing. In addition, students will need to figure out how much time should be devoted to each of these activities. By completing a project such as this, students figure out how to learn independently, as well as how to be responsible.

Almost as important to understand is what project-based learning is *not*. Simply having students participate in a hands-on activity where they produce a product other than a pencil-and-paper assessment does not necessarily constitute project-based learning. For example, if a teacher has a mock trial where all of the roles and characters have been assigned and clearly defined, then it is not a project, even though the end product looks unique from what is typically seen in the classroom. Projects must involve room for the students to discover and create for themselves.

If any of the following characteristics is missing from a lesson, then it may not be project-based learning:

- student choice,
- an open-ended question,
- a real-world problem,
- a lack of teacher-prescribed activities,
- student-led constructive investigation,
- an authentic assessment,
- student-driven time management,
- student-driven learning,
- collaborative learning,
- challenge for every student,
- student autonomy,
- independent work, or
- a conclusion featuring a product fashioned after an adult or real-world model.

Although there are many variables that can be changed within PBL—from the amount of time students have, to the resources they are given, to the product, and so on—what always remains the same is that students are given the majority of the responsibility for their own learning. PBL employs the old Confucian adage: Give a person a fish, and you feed him for a day; teach a person to fish, and he'll eat forever. We can give students information, but how enduring is that kind of learning? Like the man who has learned to fish, if a student learns *how* to get information for his or her project, then that student is equipped to gather information in the future and will feel more confident and independent about learning.

To make the mock trial assignment previously discussed into a PBL experience, a teacher could ask students to come up with a case to be argued by two teams. The students would also create the characters needed for the trial (e.g., prosecuting lawyers, defense lawyers, witnesses), hold depositions, and enact the situation in a real-world manner, which would necessitate research and preparation. This way, choice has entered into the equation, along with independent, student-driven research and authentic assessment.

There are other teaching methods out there that sound and seem very similar to PBL, such as problem-based learning and inquiry-based learning. Although such terms are often used interchangeably, there are indeed differences amongst them.

Although project-based and problem-based learning have many similarities (e.g., students work to solve a problem in both styles), the biggest difference lies in where students exercise choice. In problem-based learning, the students are given a problem they have to solve. Here, they can choose the methods by which they arrive at the solution, but generally, the problem is prescribed for them. In project-based learning, there may not be a specific problem—the project may involve simply learning more about a topic—and students have a lot of control over not only the direction of the project, but also which project they choose. To put it more succinctly, project-based learning begins with the solution, and problem-based learning begins with the problem. Project-based learning says that there is a specific solution the student must produce that shows what that student has learned, whether via a presentation, a display, a performance, or a different type of product. Problem-based learning poses a problem and charges students with finding a solution. Although problem-based learning is extremely useful in some settings (such as medical school), it poses issues in some classrooms, because students have to meet specific learning standards. Once a teacher begins structuring a problem-based approach to incorporate learning standards, it begins to resemble project-based learning.

Inquiry-based learning also involves a lot of choice. In fact, in this approach, learning is so open that there is usually no prescribed target toward which students are heading. They are simply letting their curiosity drive their learning and going wherever it takes them. This fosters a lot of creativity and higher level thinking, because students are not simply following a marked path—they are exploring and learning for themselves. Project-based learning definitely has an end goal in mind. This is important because it acts as the rudder to steer the student in the direction of learning. Consider the example of writing a book. If an author wrote a book with no ending in mind, the book would have chapters that meandered or went in directions that made no sense in terms of the overall story. If the author had the ending in mind, however, everything that he or she wrote would have a purpose, serving to deliver the reader to the conclusion. Although inquiry-based learning is valuable in some settings (the writer in this analogy would perhaps discover material for a novel that would otherwise never have been written, for instance), most classrooms require more structure in order for students to meet certain requirements and develop as learners.

Project-based learning has many aspects in common with inquiry-based learning and problem-based learning. All of these are valuable teaching and learning methods, providing students with choice and space to learn, but project-based learning provides arguably the best method of grounding learning while still allowing students to stretch their capabilities.

WHY USE PROJECT-BASED LEARNING IN THE GIFTED CLASSROOM?

There has been a big push recently for 21st-century skills. This involves students being able to do more than the memorization of knowledge, and instead applying these skills and more importantly, having the ability to problem solve (Stoof, Martens, Van Merriënboer, & Bastiaens, 2002). Businesses have been complaining the best and brightest the educational system is sending their way are very intelligent but woefully inept at figuring out problems, arguing students know a lot of "facts," but are not "competent" (Bastiaens & Martens, 2000).

We as educators have to do a better job in preparing students to solve these real working problems. How do we do that in the current system of reading textbooks, filling out worksheets, and taking tests? How many times in your life do you have to take a test outside of an educational setting? In real life we are usually dealing with projects, either at work, at home, or in other settings. If we truly want to get students ready for the real world, we should be teaching them how to handle the real world dilemma of a project.

According to the Buck Institute for Education (2011), research studies have demonstrated that project-based learning can:

- increase academic achievement on standardized assessment tests;
- teach math, economics, social studies, science, medical skills, and health-related subjects more effectively than traditional teaching methods;
- increase long-term retention of knowledge, skill development, and student and teacher satisfaction;
- prepare students to integrate and explain concepts better than traditional instructional methods;
- prove especially helpful for low-achieving students;
- present a workable model for larger school reform; and
- help students to master 21st-century skills such as communication, independent and critical thinking, and research.

This is why project-based learning is such a good fit for gifted education, which is charged with the difficult task of being more stimulating and comprehensive than traditional instruction. Teachers with gifted students have to do high quality work with these students precisely because gifted students are *capable* of doing more; PBL allows students to work to their full capabilities.

It is well documented that gifted students prefer to structure their own tasks and establish their own deadlines, as opposed to being assigned tasks and deadlines by teachers (Dunn, Dunn, & Price, 1984; Renzulli, Smith, & Reis, 1982; Stewart, 1981). There have been studies that showed that gifted students learned more and retained content more accurately when allowed to work on projects where they were setting the pace (Whitener, 1989). Research has also indicated that there is an increased benefit in learning when gifted students teach each other through projects (Johnsen-Harrris, 1983; Kingsley, 1986). Another benefit of PBL for gifted students is that when working in groups, students develop cooperative learning skills as they work together to solve problems (Peterson, 1997). Even in subjects for which it might seem more difficult to use project-based learning (e.g., mathematics), students engaged in PBL have performed better than those students taught using traditional methods (Grant & Branch, 2005; Horton, Hedetniemi, Wiegert, & Wagner, 2006; Johnston, 2004; Jones & Kalinowski, 2007; Ljung & Blackwell, 1996; McMiller, Lee, Saroop, Green, & Johnson, 2006; Toolin, 2004). In a study of two secondary schools, one project-based, the other more traditional,

> Students at the project-based school performed as well or better than students at the traditional school on items that required rote knowledge of

mathematical concepts, and three times as many students at the project-based school as those in the traditional school attained the highest possible grade on the national examination. (Thomas, 2000, p. 31)

Based on all of these data, we might ask ourselves not why we *should* use project-based learning, but rather why we would ever *not* choose to use project-based learning, given its results and benefits.

THE NEW THREE R'S

The original three R's for education were:
- reading,
- writing, and
- arithmetic.

These were already a bit of a stretch, considering that only one of them actually begins with the letter R. Contrast these educational tenets with those of project-based learning, which all start with R:
- readiness,
- responsibility, and
- relevance.

Project-based learning is designed to teach students these three R's, all valuable life skills.

READINESS

Readiness involves the level that the student is at when you introduce a project. There are three students, each at a different level of readiness. Student #1 is at a basic level, where he or she knows nothing and needs to grasp the initial concept. Student #2 has a basic understanding coming in and is ready to build on this understanding to go a little deeper. Student #3 has a clear understanding of the skill in question and is hitting the ground running, ready to take the project in related directions and further knowledge. Even when working with gifted students, you will run into this range of levels, although more students than in a typical classroom may already be at the level of Student #3. One of the most beneficial aspects of PBL is that students at all three of these levels can work on the same project—each at the appropriate level of readiness.

According to Matthews and Foster (2005), "Project-based learning experiences . . . have many benefits for diverse learners" (p. 117). PBL is inherently tiered in its design, because the students can create products at their individual skill levels. Student #1 creates a product that displays a basic level, Student #2 creates something that shows more growth, and Student #3, the student many of your gifted students likely resemble, creates a more complex product that displays deep understanding. A uniform lecture-based unit culminating in a pencil-and-paper test typically will not offer the flexibility that allows gifted students to rise above expectations. On such a test, students either respond correctly, or they do not.

The natural differentiation that PBL creates allows each student to gain skills and knowledge at the pace and level that is best suited to his or her needs.

Differentiation and scaffolding are terms that we toss around in the gifted world, but in practice, they remain difficult for some teachers to employ. Rather than truly differentiating, some teachers simply throw more work at the gifted student, which causes that student to resent being labeled as gifted. Project-based learning allows for a fairly simple method of differentiating, wherein the student sets the level for what can be accomplished.

RESPONSIBILITY

In addition to providing opportunities for differentiation, PBL teaches the valuable skill of responsibility. Think about the vast chasm between high school responsibility and college responsibility. For the most part, high school teachers enforce responsibility with discipline: detention, phone calls to parents, oral threats, poor grades, and so on. If a student skips a class, that student may be referred to a truant officer. Most high schoolers are still legally children and thus are treated as such, with most of the responsibility being put upon the adults who regulate their progress. In college, the consequences of irresponsibility are bad grades and potentially being kicked out of school. The only warnings college students generally receive are letters from administrative offices. If a college student misses a class, no one is there to hand the student make-up work during the following class, or to call home to see why the student was missing. College students are technically—and suddenly—adults, and are left to fend for themselves, like baby birds pushed from the nest and expected to fly.

Yet high school is supposed to prepare students for college. The problem with this is that in most cases, high school places the responsibility for learning on the teacher, whereas college places that responsibility on the student. The disparity between these philosophies can cause a lot of problems for new college students trying to adjust. Switching from high school to college is like training someone how to drive a car using an automatic, and then switching to a standard car for the driving test. The best way to prepare somebody for a given situation is to use the same conditions that they will experience in that situation. Why not teach students the responsibility they will need at an earlier age so that their transition to college is a smooth one, rather than jarring? Why even wait until high school to do this? If we teach children in elementary school to be responsible for their learning, then it will be embedded in them. Primary and secondary schools need to do a better job of teaching children how to fish for themselves, rather than just handing them fish. Students must learn responsibility in order for this shift in learning to occur.

Even for students who are not planning to go to college, responsibility will have to be learned at some point. If somebody misses a deadline or misses too many days of work, that person may be fired. If somebody doesn't pay the bills, there are negative repercussions—the electricity gets shuts off, or possessions are taken away. Responsibility is an important life skill that is often shocking to young adults when they enter the real world. If we taught students responsibility earlier, it would prepare them for the real world while also empowering them to learn independently.

Project-based learning puts the brunt of the responsibility for learning on the students. The teacher is there to guide them if they get stuck, or put them back on track if they become confused, but students must determine for themselves when to do what, how much time to spend on a given skill, and where to look for what they need.

In PBL, here are some of the responsibilities given to the students:

- **Task prioritization.** Students must break down a project to determine what is needed in order for them to complete it. By doing this, students prioritize tasks and then figure out how to complete them.
- **Time management.** Students must choose how to manage their time. How much time do they need for each skill or task? They have to decide what needs to be done first, and by what date, so that enough time is left for them to complete the remaining tasks. They must also manage their time in the way that best suits their own strengths and needs.
- **Learning strengths.** Students must figure out what their strengths of learning are. Are they strong researchers who are good at finding pertinent information in a sea of misleading sources, or do they need the simplicity of a textbook to lay down the basics in a plain, clear-cut manner? Or would their skills be better utilized in an interview, where they could ask very specific questions and use interpersonal skills? Discovering their learning styles and strengths allows students to guide their own learning experiences.
- **Product choice.** Which product will best display what the students have learned, while at the same time playing to their strengths? If the student is a talented writer, an essay would be the logical choice of product, whereas if the student is a good public speaker, then a speech would make more sense. A student with a lot of technology skills may opt to create an interactive website. It falls to the students to choose their product, and this sort of ownership will make them more enthusiastic about their products.

In a traditional classroom, a teacher provides all of these responsibilities—but in a PBL classroom, the students are fishing for themselves. They may stumble—miscalculating how much time they need for a given task, for instance, or choosing a product that is too advanced—but learning from these mistakes is more valuable then having everything handed to them. Knowing one's own strengths and limitations is integral to being a good learner.

RELEVANCE

How many times has a student asked, while working on a lesson, "What does this have to do with me?" Sure, we can claim that a given skill or subject will be useful further on down the road, but students rarely think in terms of the future. (Moreover, it is possible that what they are learning in a traditional classroom will *not* serve to help them in the real world.) Project-based learning is relevant even if a student feels that a project's subject matter is not applicable to his or her life or interests, because the methods used to *learn* the subject matter—namely, research, communication, and teamwork—are unquestionably relevant.

Think about your own life. Do you need school to learn how to operate your latest gadget, or to assemble a piece of furniture from IKEA? Does a teacher have to assign you a book to read before you'll pick it up and read it on your own because it seems interesting? We do not need schools to learn—we learn things in our everyday lives without the benefits of school. People learn things for their own benefit: to be able to do useful things, to better understand topics that interest them, and to prepare for situations that require certain skills. Project-based learning, more so than traditional learning, enables students to learn in a more naturalistic way, exploring subjects at their own pace and in ways that suit their interests and ambitions.

Students who are given a PBL assignment must discover for themselves where to search for information. They need to determine whether the most useful information for their purposes can be found on the Internet, from speaking to an expert, or from watching a documentary. Whichever resources they choose, they are figuring out how to learn on their own. Having these researching skills is part of teaching students to fish for themselves. If students learn to find information for themselves, rather than being passively fed information, then they will be more likely to seek out information for themselves later on for other topics, and they will feel empowered because they guided their own learning.

PROVIDING STUDENTS WITH CHOICE

One of the most valuable things project-based learning does is provide students with choice. This element of choice is a very important part of the learning process, because it recognizes students as partners in their own learning. In traditional classrooms, many students have figured out how to play the game of school: memorize the facts long enough to take the test, and then discard those facts to make room for the next set of seemingly useless information. Students are not to blame for their passivity and lack of interest. This is the system that our schools have created, and students are just working within the system. Students become so used to playing this game that often, they stop becoming engaged even when a given topic interests them.

In this way, students' natural passion for learning diminishes, because every aspect of learning becomes obligatory. Many teachers complain that the older their students get, the less passionate they are about learning. This is not true. Students are still passionate, but their passion is redirected into other avenues. This passion causes a student to spend countless hours trying to beat his favorite video game. This passion influences a student to work on her tennis game every morning before school. This passion gets some students to learn everything they can about their favorite bands, computer programming, or cooking. A student's passion may even be channeled into getting out of doing work—typical among underachieving gifted students. Passion is what drives students to devote endless hours to learning about things that may seem useless to us, but that are fascinating to them. What makes these students so passionate? It is that they *chose* what to be passionate about.

Here are some of the aspects of learning that vary within a PBL classroom, providing students with choice:

- the topics students explore,
- the products students make,
- the types of research students conduct,
- how students manage their time,
- how students are assessed,
- whether students work alone or in groups, and
- whether students fail.

The final item in this list probably threw you for a loop, but in reality, students choose to fail all of the time. They choose not to get their work done, or they choose not to be responsible. It is important for students to understand that by making certain choices, they are in fact choosing to fail. This does not mean that you, the teacher, are giving up on a student who fails. It is important to make the distinction between failing and *choosing* to fail, especially among underachieving gifted students. How many times have you heard students claim that their teacher *gave* them a failing grade? Here, the impetus of failure is being placed on the teacher, and the student is refusing to accept responsibility. In the student's mind, the teacher was responsible for imparting the information, so why shouldn't the teacher also be responsible for the failure? In a PBL classroom, students are responsible both for learning and for success—or failure. For this reason, teachers in PBL classrooms often use contracts with students to remind them of their responsibilities. Just like contracts in the real world, the learning contract exists to remind the students of what is expected. If the student fails, then it is clear who has failed and why.

Having choices usually motivates students. If they feel that they have some choice in a project, then they are more likely to be excited about the project and will work harder as a result. As Karen Rogers (2002) stated in her book *Re-Forming Gifted Education: How Parents and Teachers Can Match the Program to Their Child*,

> matching a child's preferences for how she learns with how the curriculum is actually delivered almost certainly will enhance the child's motivation to learn so that attitudes toward school remain positive. Positive attitude and motivation are important if the student is to reach higher achievement. (p. 278)

Many times in language arts, teachers choose a book for the entire class to read. Every student is required to read this book, and all of the students must move at the same pace. We know from countless research studies that same-grade students read at different levels. Can we be surprised if imposing this artificial uniformity upon students yields poor results, leaving some students struggling and others bored? Contrast this with a classroom in which students are given 3 weeks, during which time each student chooses a book and produces a product. Some students would undoubtedly put it off until the last minute, but others would read the book in a single week and use their passion—fueled by choice—to create a wonderful product. Some teachers would be appalled at the notion of 30 students reading 30 different books. How would they have class discussion? How would teachers quiz students to ensure that they were reading their books if teachers had possibly never read the books themselves?

It is sometimes difficult for teachers to transition to project-based learning, but we must remind ourselves of the ultimate goal, which is to have students learn on their own. In the traditional classroom, the book chosen by the teacher would probably appeal to some of the students, and the pace would probably be appropriate for some students, too. But if each student chose his or her own book and product, then not only would all of the students at least have the *opportunity* to be interested, but they would also be employing real-world skills such as time management in order to reach their goals. Additionally, when students are responsible for presenting books that their fellow students have not read, their discussions are potentially more impassioned, given that they are describing something new, rather than reviewing something out of obligation. In my own classroom, I have conducted literary discussions where more than 60 students were all reading different books. What was amazing about the resulting discussions was that students were learning about different books from fellow students and were becoming interested in reading those books, as well.

Whitney and Hirsch (2007) put forth four central tenets of learning—the "four C's"—in their book *A Love for Learning: Motivation and the Gifted Child*. One of these is *control*. They noted, "meaningful differentiation of classroom instruction allows these children a sense of control. Once a learning task is established, students may be given the freedom to choose among a variety of attractive alternatives to accomplish the goal" (p. 27). This choice is what ignites passion in students, and passion is invaluable in life-long growth. After all, a person can be motivated without being passionate, but there is no passion without motivation. Giving students a passion for learning will motivate them to do well. Incorporating choice into their learning is a step in this direction.

IN A NUTSHELL

Project-based learning provides a valuable option for teachers because it allows students to become not just learners, but life-long learners. Arming students with the three R's—readiness, responsibility, and relevance—will better prepare them for college and for life in the real world, spheres where they will have to learn without being given the answers.

One of the most important aspects of the project-based learning process is allowing students to choose. This choice serves as a natural motivator and allows students to feel empowered in their learning because they have some say in what and how they learn. The specific areas in which students have choice are up to the teacher, but by providing choice, the teacher also provides greater passion for learning.

2

Creating Ownership With Calendars, Contracts, and Rubrics

INTRODUCTION

One of the greatest benefits that project-based learning provides for gifted students—or any students, for that matter—is the idea of ownership of learning. Many times in schools, we put the onus of learning squarely on the shoulders of the teacher and expect him or her to lead the students to knowledge. What if instead, we allowed the students to find the knowledge for themselves—and maybe even to develop a thirst for knowledge, making them eager to find more? This chapter will teach you how to purposefully develop student ownership through the use of backwards building, contracts, calendars, and rubrics.

HOW DO YOU TEACH OWNERSHIP?

Responsibility and student ownership are key to project-based learning, but they do not happen spontaneously, with the flip of a switch. Responsibility, like anything else, must be taught, especially to young students who have trouble getting dressed in the morning or remembering to brush their teeth.

Perhaps even more than typical children, gifted children struggle with time management. According to the Council for Exceptional Children (2010),

> Gifted kids find it especially difficult to manage their time. When a child is so interested and stimulated by her world, school projects . . . can easily become overwhelming. Highly motivated minds may tend towards perfectionism and idealism, leading many gifted kids to overcommitment and even burnout.

One reason that gifted students often struggle to manage their time is that they are able to coast through their first few years of school without being challenged. Instead of having to learn self-management skills that other students need in order to succeed, gifted students use their good memories and fast processing skills to succeed and do not learn note taking or other valuable study skills that would help with time management (Siegle & McCoach, 2005).

Organization is another issue for students, and especially for gifted kids. I cannot tell you how many times I have asked a gifted student to get something for me from a book bag or binder that, when opened, turned into an explosion of papers, books, and other assorted items shoved every which way—permission slips from years ago, homework assignments from past semesters. Because these students' minds are constantly racing, organization does not come naturally to them. This is particularly evident in younger students, although it can continue on through middle and high schools. *Self-regulation* is a term that describes student organization skills as well as students' attitudes towards executing tasks. Choice and control, both offered by project-based learning, help students to learn self-regulation skills (Zimmerman, 1989).

When teaching students responsibility and organization, there must be a clear plan in place, just as there is when teaching students anything else. Within the PBL structure, certain tools help cultivate responsibility and organization by creating ownership for the student.

CALENDARS

Because students are given a prescribed length of time to work on a project, it is always a good idea to provide each student with a blank calendar. They can use this calendar to break down the project and figure out what needs to be done by when. Breaking things down in this fashion also makes things seem more manageable for students who feel overwhelmed by large projects. The calendar breaks the whole project into smaller, more controllable pieces. Some gifted students have difficulty doing this on their own, because they may not be linear thinkers. So much is going on in their minds that they cannot figure out what steps it will take, and in what order, to reach their end product. They tackle an assigned project as a comprehensive entity, which makes the task more difficult than it has to be. The calendar prompts students to create a list of tasks that must be accomplished in order for the project to be completed.

For instance, if Michael has chosen to create a presentation using PowerPoint to demonstrate what he has learned about the accomplishments of Martin Luther King, Jr., and he has 2 weeks to do this, then he will have to break down what he needs to accomplish. The best way for Michael to do this is by using *backwards building*. Backwards building uses the model established by Wiggins and McTighe (2001) and involves starting with the end in mind. It looks like this:

Backwards Building Process
1. First, identify what will be accomplished.
2. Determine what product will best show what you have learned.
3. Plan how you will develop and execute this product.

You might sit down with Michael and counsel him on how backwards building works. In this case, you would help him to identify what he wants to accomplish, which is a presentation based on Martin Luther King, Jr. Michael has determined that the product he is going to create will be a PowerPoint presentation. To plan and execute the project, Michael will need a computer. Before he can begin to create the product, however, he needs information on Martin Luther King, Jr., which he will have to get through research. In order to reach his goal, Michael should list in backwards order the tasks he will have to complete. These are:

4. Deliver PowerPoint presentation.
3. Practice PowerPoint presentation.
2. Create PowerPoint presentation.
1. Research Martin Luther King, Jr.

Michael has a 2-week period in which to accomplish his tasks, and he must budget his time according to how long he believes each step of the plan will take. You might sit down with him and a calendar and teach him to start from the end and work his way back, beginning with the end product:

Day 1	Day 2	Day 3	Day 4	Day 5
Day 6	Day 7	Day 8	Day 9	Day 10 Present PowerPoint

You might suggest to him the importance of practicing the PowerPoint and leaving time to make adjustments:

Day 1	Day 2	Day 3	Day 4	Day 5
Day 6	Day 7	Day 8 Practice PowerPoint w/ audience	Day 9 Make any adjustments to PowerPoint	Day 10 Present PowerPoint

This will give Michael 7 days to divide up the tasks of creating the PowerPoint and doing the necessary research. At this point, he must determine how much time he will need and budget accordingly. If he is very good with PowerPoint, it may only take him a couple of days to create his presentation, and his calendar will look like this:

Day 1 Research MLK	Day 2 Research MLK	Day 3 Research MLK	Day 4 Research MLK	Day 5 Research MLK
Day 6 Create PowerPoint	Day 7 Create PowerPoint	Day 8 Practice PowerPoint w/ audience	Day 9 Make any adjustments to PowerPoint	Day 10 Present PowerPoint

Perhaps Michael is just beginning to learn PowerPoint, or perhaps he is a slower worker. In that case, he creates his calendar to accommodate for this:

Day 1 Research MLK	Day 2 Research MLK	Day 3 Research MLK	Day 4 Create PowerPoint	Day 5 Create PowerPoint
Day 6 Create PowerPoint	Day 7 Create PowerPoint	Day 8 Practice PowerPoint w/ audience	Day 9 Make any adjustments to PowerPoint	Day 10 Present PowerPoint

It is a good idea for you to recommended progress points to students. On a calendar, they would look something like this:

Day 1 Research MLK	Day 2 Research MLK **(1/2 done by end of day)**	Day 3 Research MLK	Day 4 Research MLK	Day 5 Create PowerPoint
Day 6 Create PowerPoint **(1/2 done by middle of class)**	Day 7 Create PowerPoint	Day 8 Practice PowerPoint w/ audience	Day 9 Make any adjustments to PowerPoint	Day 10 Present PowerPoint

This allows Michael to know if he is falling behind. If, for instance, he has reached Day 6 and is not halfway done with the PowerPoint, then he knows he needs to step up his efforts and catch up. Finally, you may recommend that Michael use actual dates in his calendar, so there is no confusion what Day 2 of the project is, or what Day 7 is. The calendar would then look like this:

May 11 Research MLK	May 12 Research MLK **(1/2 done by end of day)**	May 13 Research MLK	May 14 Research MLK	May 15 Create PowerPoint
May 18 Create PowerPoint **(1/2 done by middle of class)**	May 19 Create PowerPoint	May 20 Practice PowerPoint w/ audience	May 21 Make any adjustments to PowerPoint	May 22 Present PowerPoint

Creating calendars is not something that students pick up overnight. It is a skill, just like times tables and spelling, and skills must be taught and reinforced. Once students get the hang of calendars, they will begin to organize the calendars themselves, thus becoming more responsible.

To help students become accustomed to making and using calendars, it might be beneficial for you to provide a recommended calendar. It might look something like this:

MLK Project
- Research: 4 days
- Creating PowerPoint: 3 days
- Practicing and Adjusting PowerPoint: 2 days
- Present PowerPoint: 1 day

Present this calendar to students and explain that it is a *recommended* calendar. If they know they work more quickly or need more time, then they will have to adjust their own calendars. Blank calendars are included in Appendix A on pages 90–91.

You can teach the entire class at one time how to create a calendar, but once projects begin, you should conference with individual students as they are working to check their progress. If their progress does not match their calendars, discuss what modifications should be made, as well as how calendars can be changed in the future to avoid problems.

CONTRACTS

A contract is just what its name implies: an agreement between two individuals. In the case of PBL, the contract is between the student and the teacher, with the agreement that certain tasks will be accomplished. Project-based learning can be very intimidating for some students, especially if they have always been in an environment where everything has been provided for them. To give them a lot of freedom right away would be like taking a dolphin that had spent its entire existence in an artificial tank being fed by a trainer and suddenly setting it free into the wild to fend for itself. It is possible that the dolphin would not survive—and neither will students, unless you introduce them to the wilds of PBL with some guidance. Contracts provide this type of guidance, giving the students a structure to follow and making PBL a little less scary.

Contracts can be as simple or as complex as you choose to make them, so long as you teach students how to use contracts effectively. One thing that should be included in nearly every contract is the overall goal of what the student is going to accomplish. This allows the student to see the big picture and to understand how the parts add up to the whole. One potential hazard of PBL is that students can get lost in the project, spending all of their time and effort on the artwork of a comic book that is supposed to be demonstrating a scientific theory or working on the player pieces of a board game they are creating that is supposed to teach math. It is very important for students to remember their learning goals.

It is vital for the contract to have both student and teacher input sections that both parties agree on. Although you will have to walk students through the contract-making process in the beginning, the student should still be creating the parameters of the contract. This gives students ownership of the project, because they are the ones who created the objectives. If a young person's parents buy their child a car, the child may not take very good care of the car, because there is a lack of ownership—literal and figurative—over the car. If the young person worked hard, saved up money, and was responsible for monthly car payments, then the car would likely be cared for much better, because its owner would have a *sense of ownership*. Similarly, students will care more about their projects if they are the ones who create those projects and set the terms of their own success, rather than being judged on set projects according to imposed criteria.

With younger students, it is also important to get parents and guardians involved in the contract. Many parents expect that their children's education will be just like their own education. If a child doesn't come home with a worksheet or a set of problems from a book, parents may be concerned that nothing is being accomplished. PBL is foreign to them, and it is important that they understand it so that they can support their children and your efforts in the classroom. By having a parent sign off on his or her child's project, you can involve that parent in the student's learning process.

Here is an example of a simple contract:

Project Contract

Student Name: _____

Project Name: _____

Estimated Time of Project:_____
(include calendar)

Power Standard(s) Covered: _____

Other Standards Covered:

_____

_____

_____

_____

Skills Learned:

-   _____

-   _____

-   _____

-   _____

Overall Goal of Project: _____

_____

_____

Product of Project: _____

_____

Headings for Rubric Evaluation: _____

_____

(include rubric)

Student Signature: _____

Teacher's Signature: _____

Parent(s) Signature:_____

When you are discussing contracts with students, you should point out the different components of contracts. Point out the section that details which learning standards are covered, as well as the section describing the overall goal of the project. This will ensure that students keep their eyes on the prize and keep in mind their ultimate project goals. Many students are prone to losing sight of their goals due to getting too wrapped up in excitement and creativity of the project. Point out also how the contract links to the rubric that will be used to evaluate the project. This will remind students that they need to follow the requirements they set out in their rubrics when creating their products. Finally, inform students that by signing the contracts, they will become partners in learning, putting themselves in charge of their projects. The space for parents to sign is also effective in several ways. Students become more accountable as more people are made aware of their goals. Moreover, parents of gifted children tend to be very involved in their students' lives, and having them as your allies is imperative.

Once this contract has been created and signed, you should make sure that a separate copy exists for you, the student, and the parent(s). You can either make copies of the signed contract, or you can have multiple copies to be signed by all parties. Students should have their contracts on hand as they work on a project, instead of putting them away and forgetting about them. This contract is what gives students tangible ownership of their projects. Examples of different blank contracts are included in Appendix A on pages 92–93.

The use of contracts has both benefits and limitations. The University of Waterloo's Centre for Teaching Excellence (n.d.) lists the following:

BENEFITS

A learning contract:
- requires students to be intimately involved in the process of developing their unit of study;
- requires students to explore their readiness to learn and their self-directed learning skills;
- maximizes students' motivation to learn because they have chosen the agenda;
- helps to keep less independent learners on course because it is specific and concrete;
- may include a schedule of regular meetings with the advising faculty member;
- encourages independence of students—less demands made on advising faculty members' time;
- provides a formal way to structure learning goals and activities as well as evaluation of learning goals—helps to minimize misunderstandings and poorly communicated expectations;
- provides continual feedback about progress made; and
- enables advising faculty member to encourage the use of a wide variety of resources (e.g., peers, library, community, experiences).

LIMITATIONS

A learning contract:
- may be challenging to create for students who are used to lecture/exam types of courses;

- is not suitable for content with which student is totally unfamiliar—some initial guidance may be required;
- may require modification as the unit progresses—careful thought is needed for how much modification is acceptable, and this could be defined at the outset of each unit; and
- requires that faculty members redefine their traditional roles and make the transition from teacher to advisor.

As you can see, the benefits of learning contracts are many—and although they also have limitations, these limitations are surmountable with organization and proactive advising on the part of the teacher.

RUBRICS

When students are involved in the creation and completion of a project, it makes sense that they should also be involved in the evaluation of the project. In PBL, this involvement comes in the form of a rubric. In the traditional classroom, rubrics are typically created by the teacher to evaluate a project in which everyone in the class participates. In project-based learning, because students are provided much more choice regarding their products, it is nearly impossible for there to be a single rubric that covers all of the varying selections the students might make. Instead, students create their own rubrics. This way, each rubric can be tailored to the particular requirements of each project. For instance, if a student were writing a research paper, the rubric would include writing conventions such as spelling, grammar, and sentence structure. If, however, the student were giving an oral presentation, then spelling and grammar would not be applicable. Instead, the rubric would include items such as confidence in speaking, vocal projection, and eye contact with the audience.

When students create their own rubrics, to be used to evaluate their own products, they have ownership over the grades they earn. They had a say in how they would be evaluated. They were clear on what the expectations were, because they were the ones who established those expectations. This ownership is also evident in the outcome of students' products. Because the students create their own rubrics, they are more aware of the expectations and will not overlook them, as sometimes happens when the teacher creates the rubric. Some teachers opt to extend this ownership by having students evaluate their own products and performances. By creating their own rubrics—and in some situations, by self-evaluating—students experience learning very differently than they do traditionally. Not only do they become more motivated, interested, and committed, but they also become more likely to flourish.

Creating and using rubrics is an extremely important component of PBL. Chapter 7 expands on the topic of rubrics and offers step-by-step instructions on how to guide students in creating and following their own rubrics.

IN A NUTSHELL

Calendars, contracts, and rubrics are key tools for teaching students responsibility. These strategies, in a project-based learning classroom, allow students to take ownership of their learning. In order to be successful, however, calendars, contracts, and rubrics must be introduced and monitored by the teacher; they are tools that require some instruction to master, but once students are comfortable using them, they will have increased ownership over their learning and products.

3

How to Use Learning Standards and Bloom's Taxonomy With Projects

■ ■ ■ ■ ■ ■ ■ ■ ■ ■ ■ ■ ■

INTRODUCTION

In this chapter, you will learn that project-based learning and teaching students according to national and state learning standards need not be mutually exclusive. Teachers—including teachers of gifted students—can very easily incorporate a wide range of learning standards into their projects. In many cases, state and national standards actually provide focus in the PBL classroom, much in the same way that a learning contract provides students with focus. Regrettably, many state and national standards use the lowest bar possible when it comes to establishing learning objectives for students. Thus, it is useful to consider Bloom's taxonomy of learning alongside the learning standards that you must meet in your classroom, thus ensuring that your students not only meet the requisite standards, but also exceed them, taking their learning to more advanced levels.

THE USE OF STANDARDS IN TODAY'S WORLD OF TEACHING

In today's era of No Child Left Behind, teachers have more accountability than ever before. Whether you consider this increased accountability good or bad, it remains the case. Most states set up their accountability systems by creating state standards that all students in a given grade are expected to master for a given subject. Here is a sample set of Writing Applications standards for 11th graders in California (California State Board of Education, 2007):

Write job applications and résumés:
   a. Provide clear and purposeful information and address the intended audience appropriately.

b. Use varied levels, patterns, and types of language to achieve intended effects and aid comprehension.

c. Modify the tone to fit the purpose and audience.

d. Follow the conventional style for that type of document (e.g., résumé, memorandum) and use page formats, fonts, and spacing that contribute to the readability and impact of the document. (p. 71)

Teachers know that learning standards must be met, and they often complain that their lessons are in large part dictated by the standards. Many teachers believe that they must choose between standards-based learning and project-based learning, but this is not the case. Teachers can run project-based learning that is based on the standards. How easy would it be to create a project using the above standards, wherein students could be involved in a mock job fair, applying and interviewing for a position? This would put them in a real-world situation. You might even bring in real employers to interview students for a potential summer job, or ask professionals to give students feedback on their résumés and interviewing skills.

Many districts simply assume that gifted students will meet the standards no matter what; thus, they focus their attention on students who are struggling. As a teacher of gifted students, though, you are not only obligated to ensure that your students understand the basic standards, but you must also push them beyond those basic standards to achieve the deeper understanding that gifted students are capable of. You must find a way to teach using PBL while still integrating the state standards into your project-based classroom.

THE IMPORTANCE OF HAVING A CORE

Most of the work that a teacher in a project-based learning environment does consists of preparatory work, finished before the teacher even sets foot in the classroom. Much of the structure and resources of a PBL classroom must be accomplished in the planning stages. Once a project begins, a teacher adopts the role of a coach. If well planned, projects can pretty much run themselves. This is why it is important to have a learning objective at the core of your project: to keep focused. That is where state and national learning standards come into play.

Students need to be aware that although they are having fun and should be creative, they are supposed to be learning something, as well. Writing a specific learning standard into the students' contracts, or using an essential question based on a certain standard, will make clear to students what they must gain from the project. For instance, you wouldn't want a student working on a math project centered on designing a fort without realizing that by doing this, the concept of perimeter was being explored and learned. You would want the concept of perimeter to be foremost in the student's mind; designing a fort would be the vehicle used to learn the concept.

Putting specific standards at the core of the project also fends off skepticism from administrators or parents who are concerned about standardized testing. There are some administrators who are fearful of PBL because they believe that it does not prepare students for state assessment tests. Being able to show your principal precisely how your students' projects use the standards will go a long way in convincing him or her to see the value of these projects. What is more, students will not only meet the standards, but they will also understand them at a deeper level, making it likely that they will achieve higher scores as a result.

Similarly, there will be parents who dismiss projects as being creative, but not really instructive or worthwhile on an educational level. Being able to show parents how you are using state standards as the backbone for a given project reassures them that PBL is a valid and productive use of class time.

BEING AT THE PROPER LEVEL OF BLOOM'S

When incorporating learning standards into your projects, you must be sure that students master a given standard to the level that is expected. One way to understand the depth of learning that is expected by a standard—and subsequently, to ensure that students reach this level of understanding—is to use Bloom's taxonomy (Bloom, Engelhart, Furst, Hill, & Krathwohl, 1956), a well-known classification of learning objectives.* You can use the wording and context of a standard to rate it according to Bloom's taxonomy. If a standard is higher on the taxonomy, then that standard is associated with an increased depth of understanding. There are six levels in Bloom's taxonomy:

1. *Knowledge*: recalling basic facts and concepts
2. *Comprehension*: demonstrating understanding of something learned
3. *Application*: using information already learned in a new way
4. *Analysis*: breaking information into parts and examining those parts by looking for relationships
5. *Synthesis*: taking something apart and creating something new
6. *Evaluation*: judging something based on a set of criteria

Knowledge, comprehension, and application are the lower levels of thinking, whereas analysis, synthesis, and evaluation are the higher levels.

Generally, the level of Bloom's taxonomy that a learning standard expects students to reach can be determined by the verb(s) in the standard. For instance, consider the following standard, from the North Carolina Second Grade Social Studies Standards (Public Schools of North Carolina, 2006):

▪ Analyze and evaluate the effects of responsible citizenship in the school, community, and other social environments. (p. 24)

The verbs here are *analyze* and *evaluate*, both of which are higher levels of Bloom's taxonomy. Thus, you should not simply create a project wherein students participate in a community service project. That would constitute application and would represent a lower level on Bloom's taxonomy. At some point in the project you create, students will need to analyze. This may involve having students choose community service projects from a list and then making arguments for why they chose the projects they did. To meet the evaluation component of the standard, you might have students reflect on their community service experiences in order to assess how well the community engages in this service, or to explain how effective their own actions were and how they could have been more effective.

---

* Bloom's taxonomy was revised in 2001 by L. Anderson and D. A. Krathwohl; however, being that many educators are more familiar with the original taxonomy, that is the one that will be discussed in this book.

In this scenario, students would be learning at the higher level—characterized by analysis and evaluation—set forth by the standard.

Sometimes, the language used in the standard does not make it as obvious which level of Bloom's taxonomy it is associated with. Let us consider the following standard, taken from the Common Core State Standards for Grade 1, Measurement and Data (Common Core State Standards Initiative, 2010):

- Organize, represent, and interpret data with up to three categories. (par. 4)

Here, the verbs organize, represent, and interpret are not as obvious regarding their placement in Bloom's taxonomy. You will have to determine at which level of Bloom's the standard is asking students to learn. In this particular case, the standard lies primarily at the application level, with students organizing and representing what they have learned, and perhaps also falls into the analysis level with the verb *interpret*. Nothing new is being created, which is to say the standard does not reach the synthesis level.

Often, you will need to use context clues to determine the level of a standard. There are certain keywords that typically indicate where in Bloom's taxonomy a given standard lies. Here is a basic Bloom's keyword chart:

Knowledge	choose, define, find, identify, locate, recall, recognize, select, show, tell
Comprehension	add, compare, describe, distinguish, explain, express, paraphrase, rephrase, summarize, understand
Application	answer, conduct, demonstrate, design, develop, illustrate, interpret, investigate, organize, present, produce, respond, solve
Analysis	classify, compare and contrast, deduce, distinguish, edit, examine, explain, infer, reason, validate
Synthesis	combine, compile, create, hypothesize, imagine, integrate, invent, organize, rearrange, revise
Evaluation	assess, conclude, criticize, debate, give an opinion, judge, justify, prove, recommend, verify

A more complete keyword chart can be found in the Reproducibles section on page 94.

Keep in mind that sometimes a verb can apply to more than one level of Bloom's taxonomy. The verb *compare*, for instance, lies in both the comprehension and the analysis levels. If students were comparing information explicitly stated in a passage and were simply drawing conclusions, then they would be using comprehension, a lower level. If they were interpolating and making comparisons using assumptions and conclusions not explicitly mentioned in the passage, then they would be analyzing.

It may be helpful for you to create a taxonomy table for the standards that you have to cover in your subject area. A taxonomy table simply helps list the standards that must be covered (organized by strands) and provides a visual reminder of the standards' respective Bloom's levels. For instance, take the following selection of math strands from the Missouri Department of Elementary and Secondary Education (2008):

- Numbers and Operations

- Algebraic Relationships
- Geometric and Spatial Relationships
- Measurement
- Data and Probability

Here are the standards under Data and Probability for third grade (italics added for emphasis):
a. *Design* investigations to address a given question
b. *Read* and *interpret* information from line plots and graphs (bar, line, pictorial)
c. *Describe* the shape of data and analyze it for patterns
d. *Discuss* events related to students' experiences as likely or unlikely (pp. 21–23)

By using the verbs and their contexts, we can identify standards a. and b. as being at the application level, c. as being at the comprehension level, and d. as being at the evaluate level. We then organize these various standards in a taxonomy table under the strand of Data and Probability. An example of a taxonomy table with this strand completed would look like this:

Science	Knowledge	Comprehension	Application	Analysis	Synthesis	Evaluate
Numbers and Operations						
Algebraic Relationships						
Geometric and Spatial						
Measurement						
Data and Probability		c	a, b			d

You would do this for all of the standards that you had to cover. In this way, you create a map for yourself, reminding yourself of what you need to cover and in how much depth.

PROVIDING DEPTH

Many state standards are written at the lower levels of Bloom's taxonomy, those dealing with knowledge and comprehension. For example, when students memorize the Great Lakes or multiplication tables, they are working at the knowledge level. According to Bloom's taxonomy, this is the lowest level of thinking. Comprehension is just a step above knowledge and might involve a student reading a story and then summarizing the plot or learning from a passage about sound how echoes are generated.

One of the many benefits of PBL—especially with regard to gifted students, whom we seek to challenge with higher level thinking—is that simply by producing a product, students are already working at an application level, the highest of the lower thinking levels.

Sometimes a project will even ask a student to analyze, synthesize, or evaluate, the higher learning levels of Bloom's taxonomy.

Consider the following standard, taken from the ninth grade Virginia Standards of Learning in English (Virginia Department of Education, 2010):

- Identify the characteristics that distinguish literary forms. (p. 2)

In order to show mastery of this standard, a student would simply have to identify various literary forms, such as fiction, nonfiction, and poetry, making this a knowledge-level skill. But if you created a project for which students had to write samples of each type of literature—a fictional piece, a memoir piece, and a poem—then they would be *applying* the skill in addition to identifying it. Alternatively, the students could break down literary forms even further to genres such as mystery, science fiction, and historical fiction. Then they could write the same story three different ways, demonstrating the differences among the various fictional genres. This would involve synthesis thinking. Students would be meeting the same standard, but they would need to understand the same subject matter in a more nuanced and in-depth way from completing a project.

STARTING WITH THE STANDARD

So how does a teacher create a project using the standards? There are a few different ways to approach this. One way is simply to create a project for each individual standard. Take this set of eighth-grade standards from Louisiana's Content Standards, Benchmarks, and Grade Level Expectations for Science (Louisiana Department of Education, 2010):

- Demonstrate that Earth has a magnetic field by using magnets and compasses.
- Define gravity and describe the relationship among the force of gravity, the mass of objects, and the distance between objects.
- Predict how the gravitational attraction between two masses will increase or decrease when changes are made in the masses or in the distance between the objects.
- Explain the relationships among force, mass, and acceleration. (p. 34)

You could turn each of these into a separate project quite easily. A project based on the first standard could involve having students use magnets to create their own compasses (e.g., water compasses). A project based on the second standard could involve dropping various objects out of a window and measuring the speed of the drop compared to the mass of the object. The third standard could be learned with a research project about planets and gravity, while the last standard's project could be a derby, where students made their own cars of different masses and measured their acceleration.

Obviously, creating a different project for each standard would likely be very time consuming. If each student created a project for each standard, then it could take months just to cover these four standards. One way around this would be to present all four standards to the class in a more traditional format and then to have individual students choose which standards to learn about. You could put students into groups according to their interests, and then each group would be charged with teaching their assigned standard to the rest of the class. This way, each standard would be covered in a shorter timespan. If a group left out important information in its presentation, you could cover this information or call the group's attention to an aspect of the topic that needed further attention.

A second way to organize the project is to have an overarching theme. In the case of the four science standards, they all relate to the theme of motion and force. The students would create a project where they incorporated all four standards into the product. This would show not only that they understood the individual standard, but also that they understood how the standards were interrelated, demonstrating a deeper understanding.

Yet another way to cover these four standards would be to put students in groups of four. Each member of the group would then become responsible for coming up with a product that covered one of the standards. The group would present together, thereby covering all four aspects of motion and force. The advantage of covering standards in this way is that it allows students to work collaboratively. Any time students can learn to work with others, they are using real-world skills; increasingly, teamwork and its related 21st-century skills (such as incorporating constructive criticism into a project) are vital for students to learn. The disadvantages of this approach are those that typically accompany group work. A certain group member may not contribute, thus dragging everybody else down. This is where you, as the teacher in a PBL classroom, would step in as a coach. Because the teacher is not leading the class in lecture or other traditional methods, he or she is freer to counsel students in their research and manage the groups' dynamics to make sure that everyone is doing what they are supposed to be doing.

Another way you might set up a project would involve working the standard in without informing students explicitly of the standard—like putting the medicine in with the applesauce. This approach mimics the form of inquiry-based learning; you would prompt the students by writing "motion and force" on the board. Then you would have the students brainstorm ideas for various projects using their prior knowledge, listing them on the board around the initial topic. If students don't seem to have much background on the topic, you might conduct an introductory experiment or have students read a brief passage in order to gain some preliminary knowledge. Your job in this case is to refine students' suggestions and work in the standards that need to be covered. For instance, if a student mentioned Newton and his discovery of gravity by way of the apple falling on his head, you could continue to discuss this myth, working in the idea of mass. Or if students are discussing magnets and have not mentioned compasses, you might offer it up as a suggestion and see where students go with it.

Whichever of these four methods you use—or if you come up with a different way to incorporate learning standards into your projects—it is important to be sure that the learning standards act as the backbone for student learning. This way, you remain accountable with regard to the standards, but at the same time, you enable your students to learn in much greater depth.

IN A NUTSHELL

State and national learning standards should form the basis for all of your class's projects. In addition to providing students with a clear learning goal, using the standards reassures parents and administrators that students will get the education they need in order to succeed on high-stakes tests. Parents and administrators should also understand that through completing carefully planned projects, students learn standards in more depth, ensuring lasting understanding.

It can be helpful to create a taxonomy table to ensure that students are learning at the level the standard demands. Making this kind of table involves combing through the standards and identifying the level of Bloom's that each standard asks of students:

1. *Knowledge:* recalling basic facts and concepts.
2. *Comprehension:* demonstrating understanding of something learned.
3. *Application:* using information already learned in a new way.
4. *Analysis:* breaking information into parts and examining relationships.
5. *Synthesis:* taking something apart and creating something new.
6. *Evaluation:* judging something based on a set of criteria.

Once you have created a taxonomy table, you can refer to it when creating projects, being sure that students demonstrate the requisite mastery of each standard.

In order to teach the necessary learning standards in a PBL classroom, teachers can use various methods. They can:

- cover each standard with an individual project;
- group standards together by theme;
- divide the standards and have different student groups cover each one; and
- have students explore various topics on their own, filling in the blanks as needed to cover the standards.

You can use any of these methods—or a combination—to guarantee that your students learn the material that they must to meet state and national standards. With PBL, students can learn this material in more depth, incorporating valuable real-world skills.

Finding the Structure That Works for You, Your Classroom, and Your Students

INTRODUCTION

Now that you understand why you should use project-based learning in your gifted classroom, the next logical step is to figure out how. In this chapter, you will learn the various philosophies regarding how to set up PBL in your classroom. There is no single perfect formula. Every teacher has to find what works best in his or her own classroom, what is best for the students, and what works best within the curriculum. Finding the right balance can be difficult, but the adaptability of PBL means that there are many areas in which adjustments can be made so that projects benefit everyone.

KEYS TO A SUCCESSFUL PBL CLASSROOM

The key to having a successful classroom that uses project-based learning is finding the right structure: the structure that works best for you, for the students, and for learning. Finding the right structure can be like finding the right relationship: You have to kiss a few toads to find the prince. In other words, you will have to experiment to see what works and what does not work. And failing is perfectly all right—all failure means is that you have found a way that doesn't work, as Thomas Edison famously pointed out after finding 10,000 different ways that did not produce a working light bulb. Ideally, it will not take you 10,000 attempts to find the correct structure for your PBL classroom, but it is unlikely that you will find the perfect structure right off the bat. Don't be discouraged when the structure that looked perfect on paper crashes and burns when you start to use it in the classroom. You will need to make adjustments.

It is also important to understand that once you find a formula that works, you should not assume that it will work with every class. There are certain variables that may change the success or failure of that particular structure, such as the maturity of your students, the resources available to you, and the amount of content that students bring to the project. As with any long-term relationship, if you simply keep doing the same thing over and over without changing things, the relationship will begin to stagnate and sour. As a teacher, you need to be willing to make adjustments to fit your evolving situation.

For instance, imagine that a teacher begins the year with a structure that calls for students to do a certain amount of work at home. After spending a couple of months with this structure, the teacher discovers that students are not able to do the work at home without the books that the classroom provides. The teacher is going to have to adjust. She could allow the classroom books to be checked out for students to take home. She could allot more time in class for students to work on the project with the books. She might find ways to prevent students from being distracted. Or she could find websites to act as alternatives to the information provided by the books. All of these would be viable solutions to the structure's problem.

There is a formula that all structures should follow. This formula is laid out by Matthews and Foster (2005) in their book *Being Smart About Gifted Children: A Guidebook for Parents and Educators*: "When project-based learning is undertaken, the teacher should develop an appropriate framework such that learning is scaffolded and productive, and there is ongoing monitoring and guidance" (p. 117). In this description, the authors mention the terms *scaffolded*, *productive*, *monitoring*, and *guidance*. Let us take a look at these terms and determine what they mean.

SCAFFOLDED

Projects lend themselves to scaffolding because students are given a lot of choice regarding how deep they go with the learning of the topic. The projects must be set up so that gifted students can go into as much depth as they choose. This means that the project must be somewhat open ended or should allow for further research in similar areas. In the beginning, you will need to show students what is meant by deep—otherwise, you will generally get the minimum that you ask for, as students are accustomed to doing only what is required of them. You can demonstrate in-depth learning to students through suggestions and modeling.

When I am introducing projects to students, I will show them examples of products from years past that demonstrate poor, good, and excellent depth. Rather than telling the students which project is which level, I show them all three examples and ask them to evaluate the projects for themselves. Which one has the most depth, and which one has the least? Students nearly always agree with my evaluations, and in addition, they are forced to view others' projects in the same way that I (and their classmates) will view theirs. It is important to note that with projects, more work does not necessarily equate with better work. Rather, better work involves unique work, work that involves higher level thinking to address the topic at a level above and beyond that which was asked for. If, for instance, students are asked to discuss the orbit of the Earth and discuss how this relates to the passage of a year, a student might also look at the causes of a leap year, explaining why there is an extra day every 4 years. Showing students models of different-quality projects demonstrates your expectations for them. You may also clarify expectations for students when you meet with them individually, showing them possible avenues for deepening their projects. If students are studying how the colonists won the American Revolutionary War, you could suggest that a student analyze what may have happened if the British had won the war.

It is important to encourage students to expand their horizons and think about problems for which there are not necessarily easy—or any—answers. It is important for the teacher to recognize those students who tend not to push themselves to these deeper levels and to encourage them to challenge themselves. It is also important to recognize those students who do push themselves and interfere with their progress as little as possible.

PRODUCTIVE

Students should feel that they are accomplishing something. They don't like to have their time wasted any more than anyone else does. They need to feel as though they are working towards a goal. When I first began teaching PBL, students were often a little wary of projects, because most of them had stories about how the supplemental gifted teacher had made them work on projects and then they ran out of time or nothing was done with the work. They felt that their time had been wasted. You must make sure that the structure you design points students towards a goal. This is in part why using learning outcomes is so valuable: It focuses students towards a particular goal, and students will feel they have been productive when they accomplish it. For instance, let's say that you want students to understand the concepts of perimeter and volume. The project that students are working on is designing and/or creating a product that would demonstrate both of these concepts. One hypothetical student chooses to design a water park. Because she is a very creative student, she gets caught up in the product aspect of the project and loses sight of the learning goal, which is to learn about perimeter and volume. This is why conferencing with students and having teacher-approved checkpoints help to guide the student towards the learning outcome. The learning goal must remain the top priority.

MONITORING

The goal of the teacher in an ideal project-based classroom is not to teach. Let me state that again: The teacher does not teach in a project-based classroom. The students are learning for themselves. The role of the teacher is more that of a facilitator who monitors student progress. This usually involves checking in with students on a one-on-one basis. Monitoring a class rather than teaching allows the teacher to have a lot of face time with individual students, allowing that teacher to learn students' strengths and weaknesses. Rather than teaching 30 students as one large entity, teachers are able to see the students as 30 separate workers, each with unique skills and interests.

GUIDANCE

This aspect of structure goes hand in hand with the monitoring aspect. As you monitor students, it is important to guide students towards the correct path, rather than directing them. To direct students is to put them on a train track pointed down an exact path, forcing them to follow the same route as everyone else. The guide-from-the-side mentality consists of nudging students back in the correct general direction, but letting them take whichever route they choose in order to reach their destination. Some students might take a direct path, and others might weave back and forth, but guidance, as opposed to strict direction, allows students the freedom to learn. It should not be accomplished with a heavy hand, but with a more advisory tone.

So long as you include these four aspects of the structuring formula, the way you structure your project-based learning is totally up to you. It is essential, however, that whatever structure you settle on is made absolutely clear to students. They must understand their roles and what is expected of them. The clearer the structure is to them, the more effective and efficient they will be. This will be covered in more depth in Chapter 6.

FINDING A STRUCTURE THAT WORKS FOR YOU

As teachers, we all bring strengths and weaknesses to our practice. The key is not to turn our weaknesses into strengths or to reinvent the way we teach—the key is to set up our classrooms to best utilize our strengths while minimizing the instances in which our weaknesses show themselves. Thus, if you are a teacher who is very skilled at developing hands-on lessons, you should design your projects to reflect this. Run a lab with hands-on activities to introduce a new project so that students are receiving some background knowledge. If you are a teacher whose strength is lecture, employ this style of teaching during the time spent introducing the project.

At the same time, as teachers, we need to be willing to try new things and step out of our comfort zones. How else would we learn anything? We must keep in mind the three levels of learning.

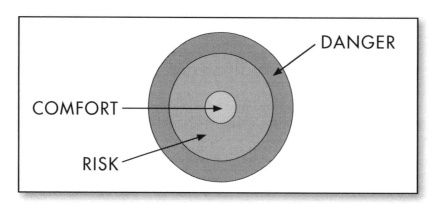

In the center, at the comfort level, there is not much learning going on. Learners are covering things that they possibly already know, and although it feels good, they are not getting much out of it. At the other extreme is the danger zone, which is just that: dangerous. If you put learners in a place where they are so unfamiliar with a subject as to be afraid of it, they will shut down and no learning will occur. Learners have to walk the precarious tightrope of the risk zone. Learners must be challenged, feeling a little uncomfortable—but not so much that they are in danger. This is the optimal place for learning to take place.

Just as we expect students to learn within this risk zone, we as teachers need to be willing to go there as well, trying methods that are outside of our comfort levels. Although you shouldn't completely reverse your usual teaching style, if you are going to attempt project-based learning, you have to be willing to stretch your comfort level.

I was a teacher who loved to lecture. I would prepare elaborate PowerPoint presentations that went on for an hour, with students developing hand cramps from taking so many notes. This was the method I had experienced throughout high school and college, and I was convinced that it worked best for students. Yet I was never satisfied with the results. Although students seemed to understand the material on a surface level, there was a disconnect between comprehension and advanced understanding. My students weren't getting the big picture.

When I switched over to project-based learning, I had to give up the hour-long lectures in order to give students time to work in class. In fact, I pledged to my class that I would never talk for more than 15 minutes at a time, even going so far as to use an egg timer set for 15 minutes. When the buzzer went off, I would stop talking. This was extremely uncomfortable at first. I felt rushed and was not getting to say all that I wanted to say. But I stuck with it and found that students paid closer attention during these 15 minutes than they had during the entire hour I had presented before. Being limited also made me more purposeful in my message, and students began to get the larger picture. I was still sticking with my strength—lecturing—but I put this strength in a different format that placed my teacher development in the risk zone, allowing me and my students to experience greater learning.

FINDING A STRUCTURE THAT WORKS FOR YOUR STUDENTS

Of course, you also need to consider your students. What are they bringing to the classroom? One would assume that gifted students bring a certain amount of knowledge and thus should love project-based learning because it allows them to explore topics in greater depth and according to their own determination. This is certainly not always the case, however, especially with some underachieving gifted students. Some of them want to find the easiest way possible to complete the task, which is rarely the best approach with projects. You need to get to know your students and see what their strengths and weaknesses are. This can be done in one-on-one conversations, with pretesting, through a learning styles inventory, with questionnaires, or using other methods. With gifted students—or any students, for that matter—you need to figure out who will need to be pushed, who will need more guidance, and who will produce superior work when given enough space.

You might run across a handful of students for whom projects simply do not work. This may be because they cannot handle the responsibility of the process, or because they need far more structure than a project gives. You have to be prepared to differentiate if necessary, giving them the more rigid structure they need (e.g., working out of a textbook, having set checkpoints). You may also try to wean these students away from these more structured methods. It is important to keep recalibrating your approach based on what you see happening in your classroom.

FINDING A STRUCTURE THAT WORKS FOR YOUR CURRICULUM

Gifted programs work in a variety of ways. Your program might be a pullout program, where you only get to see your students once a week, or you may teach gifted students periodically for sporadic enrichment, or you may teach on a team of educators and be responsible for a specific area. Whichever situation you find yourself in, you will have to create the structure that best fits the situation. I have done project-based learning in all three of these situations and find that I must use a different approach in each situation. In the pullout program, when I had students once a week, I had to be very mindful that the structure allowed students to stay focused on the project, and that they did not forget about the project during the 6 days until I saw them again. I used calendars to help keep them focused and formed contracts with them to remind them of their commitment to the program. Every week when they came back to class, we started with one-on-one conferences to check their calendars to ensure that they were on schedule. I also required students to work on their projects for at least 15 minutes every single day, working these additional blocks into their calendars, so when they came back to class after a week, they weren't trying to remember what it was they had been doing. They remained connected to the project all week long. I also extended the timespan of the projects, because we were only meeting once a week, allowing them to take 3 or 4 weeks on a project that might have taken a week or so if I were seeing them every day. For an example of the structure I used, see pages 107–111 in Appendix B.

When I had students sporadically for enrichment, I had to work with the regular classroom teachers and offer projects that we all felt would enhance the learning of the students. I also had the opportunity to offer projects in all four subject areas. Because I knew that the students were already covering the requisite learning standards in their regular education classes, I had to structure projects so that students were going far beyond the standards and getting at content in a much deeper way. Because I was not as beholden to the standards, I also taught some projects that I thought would improve students' responsibility and other life-long learning skills.

For the team approach, I had to stick to a specific subject. I was teaching science and social studies with two other teachers handling language arts and math. In addition, I was seeing the students for each subject only every other day: social studies one day, science the next. The structure had to take into account the 2 days between classes. Projects were designed for students to do far more work in class than they did in the pullout program where I was only seeing them once a week. I was able to provide resources that allowed students to work at a deeper level and counsel them further to reach the higher levels of thinking. Because I was teaching two content areas, I also varied the project structure in each. The social studies project was far more inquiry based, with students choosing topics they wanted to learn about, forming groups, and teaching their topics to the class. The science project was more tightly connected to the standards, with me providing specific objectives but allowing the students their choice of product. Students either worked by themselves or worked in pairs. For an example of the science structure, see pages 105–106 Appendix B.

The way your gifted program or your classroom is set up might limit your structure or cause you to have to adjust the way you conduct PBL. It has to be a good fit in all respects—don't try to fit a square peg into a round hole. You'll only end up frustrated.

IN A NUTSHELL

Finding the right project-based structure for your gifted classroom can seem like an overwhelming task. Whatever structure you choose needs to allow for:
- scaffolding,

- productivity,
- monitoring, and
- guidance.

It is also important to find the best fit for:
- your own strengths as a teacher;
- the strengths and limitations of your students, both as individuals and as a group; and
- your classroom and schedule.

It is often challenging to find a PBL structure that addresses all of these needs. The good news is that—as you will find out in the next chapter—there are many aspects of PBL that can be adjusted to fit your situation, so the structure you end up choosing will be malleable, allowing you to make changes to fit your purposes.

5

Ways to Vary the Structure of Projects

INTRODUCTION

There are fives aspects of project-based learning that can be varied on spectrums. Figuring out where you want to be on these spectrums is a matter of trial and error, considering the various needs of you, your students, and the curriculum. As you consider the different variables of PBL, you will have to determine where on the spectrum you want your class to be, and whether being at this point on the spectrum will accomplish what you desire for your students.

THE DIFFERENT SPECTRUMS OF PROJECT-BASED LEARNING VARIABLES

There are several different ways to vary the structure of projects in the classroom. Here are the five aspects you can vary:

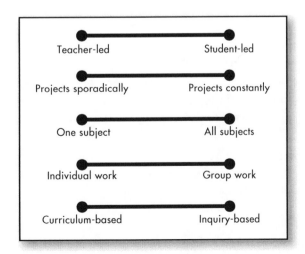

Each of these variables has two obvious extremes (e.g., student-led vs. teacher-led). Because each variable is a spectrum, however, you do not have to be at one end or the other. You can be in the middle, a little to the left, a little to the right—wherever you feel will be best for you and your students. Project-based learning is so useful largely because it is so adjustable. The fact that so many combinations exist of variables and placements on their spectrums means—again—that it will take you some time to find the ideal recipe for your classroom.

TEACHER-LED VERSUS STUDENT-LED

This aspect of PBL concerns how much involvement the teacher has in the day-to-day activities of the projects. If the project is teacher-led, then the teacher is involved in most aspects of the project—providing background information, giving specific direction, or offering direct instruction. This might be a good option for students first being introduced to project-based learning. You certainly don't want to just throw them into the deep end of the pool without any direction. You might suggest products, guide them to particular resources, or arrange for mini-lessons along the way to keep students focused and on track. At the same time, you will eventually want to wean students off of too much teacher-led instruction, or you will risk compromising the independence that students need for effective project-based learning. Once students are familiar with the structure of the project, you can go to the other end of the spectrum and have the students decide for themselves regarding factors such as time allotment, product choice, and resources, or stay in the middle and do a mixture of both.

When I am deciding where on this spectrum a given class will fall, I take into account the amount of prior knowledge that students possess. For instance, I might approach a project concerning Mesopotamia very differently than I would a project about Egypt. Students usually know very little about the cradle of civilization, Mesopotamia, so I might begin the project with a brief lecture on some of the key features of the river valley civilization, or perhaps show a documentary on some of these people's accomplishments, just to get students interested. I might also need to help students by bringing in books from the library concerning Mesopotamia or bookmark some helpful websites, as many online resources concerning Mesopotamia are university- or museum-run and may be above the heads of younger students. However, students typically bring a lot of prior knowledge concerning Egypt to the classroom. They know the staples of mummies, pyramids, the Nile, and pharaohs. So the teacher-led lecture wouldn't be necessary. There are also plenty of student-friendly resources and websites concerning Egypt, so students would need very little guidance where research was concerned.

A good way to gauge students' prior knowledge is through the use of a pretest, an interest inventory, or journaling to unpack their knowledge. Unpacking is simply allotting 15–30 minutes for students to write, sketch, or diagram all of the information they know about the topic. Sometimes students will even surprise themselves with how much they know once they begin thinking about it.

Most effective project-based learning should be on the right side (student-led) of this spectrum. There are exceptions, as mentioned, such as rigorous content or maybe a group of students that shows a lack of maturity or responsibility, requiring more discipline in order to be successful. The more comfortable you get with the PBL process, the more willing you will be to turn over the majority of the learning to the students.

PROJECTS SPORADICALLY VERSUS PROJECTS CONSTANTLY

Most teachers see the value of project-based learning. They know that if you gave one student a book chapter to read and another student a project to complete, the enduring understanding would more than likely be achieved by the student completing the project, because that student would be a stakeholder in the learning process. However, some teachers remain traditional in their methods and like to rely on memorization, pop quizzes, lectures, and other such pedagogy. They are willing to try project-based learning only here and there, and only with a specific type of lesson. When I began using projects in my classroom, I would sprinkle them in here and there. I started with easy projects, such as taking parts of the Constitution and making Schoolhouse Rock-like songs to teach about that section. I would show students examples of the Schoolhouse Rock videos, such as the "I'm Just a Bill," using these as examples of how to set up their own projects. I thought that the project was a moderate success, and I saw students having a good time, but I didn't realize the long-term impact of the project until 4 years later, when I ran into one of my students at the grocery store. There, in the middle of the condiment aisle, he sang for me his song dealing with the judiciary branch as though he had just performed it the day before. It had stuck with him. If I had drilled and killed that topic with him, he would probably have forgotten it the following week, but instead, he kept his Constitution song with him for life.

Realizing the impact that this single project had had on students, I began to use more and more projects, and I saw an increase in students' motivation, enduring understanding, and—thankfully for my principal—test results. It took me another couple of years, but I eventually converted all of my lessons into projects, effectively making my classroom exclusively a project-based classroom. I find project-based learning to be far more effective than the traditional classroom methods I used to use, and I notice results that cannot be summarized by a few humorous anecdotes—rather, I see improvement across the board in my students' enthusiasm, retention, and achievement scores.

You may choose to mix in projects with your usual methods. The advantage to this is that some students do not thrive in a project-based environment. This type of student may not push him- or herself when given the opportunity, or may lack the responsibility to handle so much independence. Some students do better sitting in rows, reading from a textbook, and answering lower level questions.

Balancing project-based and traditional instruction methods also serves to prevent student burnout. Projects can be very demanding, especially for those students who may bite off more than they can chew and then have to expend a lot of energy finishing their projects. (Gifted students, many of whom tend towards perfectionism, are often loathe to fall short of their project goals.) Breaking up projects with periods of traditional instruction can prevent this burnout and give students an occasional change of pace. Doing anything over and over again can become tedious. Even with the sort of variety a project allows, endless projects can become tiresome, and students will cease to be stimulated by projects if that is all they are exposed to.

In Montessori schools all over the world, project-based learning is the consistent learning method. Students are given a checklist of items to accomplish over the course of the week, and it falls to them to manage their time. There are items scattered around the room for students to use to help learn the concepts, but they are learning on their own with encouragement from other students. Because this is the classroom environment all of the time, students do not even blink when working on their plans; to them, this is simply the way things are done.

Ideally speaking, making your classroom exclusively a project-based learning environment is the way to go. (This runs counter to what I have already said about mixing project-based and traditional approaches in your classroom, but few classrooms nowadays are ideal for project-based learning, being that students have grown up being taught with traditional teaching methods.) This way, you do not have to devote a lot of time to teaching students how to complete projects. Students already know what is expected of them and what to expect from the project and thus can move seamlessly from project to project. Beginning with PBL, switching to a regular style of teaching during the next unit, and then returning to projects can make for clumsy transitions. Students and teachers must shift gears, and time may be lost. If projects are an everyday occurrence in your classroom, then students can simply get down to the business of learning without experiencing the awkwardness of these changes. Purposeful time will need to be spent at the beginning of the year setting up and explaining to students the project-based classroom, but once this has been done, students usually get into the swing of things, and little review for processes will be needed.

ONE SUBJECT VERSUS ALL SUBJECTS

Some subject areas lend themselves better to projects than others. This is because the learning standards associated with these subjects already suggest a certain amount of depth, allowing students to explore the topic. For instance, consider the following first-grade social studies standard from the Connecticut State Department of Education (2009):

- Examine Native American culture through books and art. (p. 5)

It would be fairly easy to come up with a project-based lesson for this, either having students research their own books and art to create a portfolio, or having students create their own Native American-inspired art based on information about the cultures of the various groups.

Math always presents more of a challenge for crafting projects. Making a meaningful project involving math—which many times is lower level in nature and not subject to much interpretation—can be difficult at times. Take another first-grade math standard from Connecticut (Connecticut Math Standards, 2010):

- Determine half of a whole set of up to 20 objects. (par. 7)

This seems pretty straightforward. All a student has to do in order to meet this standard is look at 20 crayons and determine that half of 20 is 10. How do you make a project out of this standard? It can be done—you simply have to be a little creative. Instead of having students perform the task, you could have them create a math problem sheet with 10 problems all modeled on this concept. That way, they would be creating instead of just comprehending. You could combine this concept with several others so that students would have to do multiple tasks and determine which one was the correct fit. For instance, take these additional standards from Connecticut (Connecticut Math Standards, 2010):

- Solve contextual problems using all addition sums to eighteen and subtraction differences from ten with flexibility and fluency.
- Determine and compare sets of pennies and dimes valued up to $1.00; trade sets of pennies for dime and vice versa. (par. 8)

You might have students create their own store where they will price items. When other students come to shop, they must first divide items in half in order to figure out the price, and items can be sold for play money. This will involve students using the concepts of addition, subtraction, and money identification from the other standards. Students will then be putting these math concepts into a real-world context, and they will have fun as well.

One approach that seems fairly simple is to have students develop their own lesson plans and implement them with other students using worksheets, overheads, PowerPoint presentations, or whatever products they choose. As educators, we know that in order to teach something, one has to possess a decent understanding of it in order to explain it to others. By having students teach the material, you can push them to a higher level of learning, because they must take a lower level concept and synthesize the relevant information, making the jump to higher level concepts.

Depending on what grade level you teach, you may also be able to incorporate many different subject areas into a project. An elementary teacher typically teaches all four core subject areas. If you decide to incorporate PBL into your classroom, you need not coordinate your project with any other teachers (although obviously, you will need to discuss your new approach with the administration and gain approval). However, once you move into middle school and high school levels, teachers become more specialized. Each teacher likely teaches just one subject area—two at most—so having students work on an interdisciplinary project could mean collaborating with other teachers.

There are entire schools devoted to project-based learning. The Explore Knowledge Academy is a charter school in Las Vegas that focuses on project-based learning for grades K–12. According to the Explore Knowledge Academy (2006),

- Students complete projects in which they incorporate the curriculum standards for the courses in which they are enrolled.
- They select areas of interest that are relevant to them and create an essential or guiding question to frame the investigative process.
- A minimum of three resources is required to frame student research that includes primary, secondary, and tertiary resources (i.e., texts, websites, human experts, original factual documents and accounts).
- Each project concludes with a presentation to an audience to illustrate what has been learned.
- Students then enter evidence of the learning, which includes a reflection, pictures and images, or an essay in their portfolios.
- Students must take responsibility for learning the curriculum standards for their courses, with the advisor acting as the learning coach to guide them to a higher level of work than they would produce on their own. (Project Based Learning section)

Indianapolis has both public and charter schools that focus on PBL. In the public school system of Lawrence Township, elementary schools have switched over to project-based learning on a district-wide basis, with two of the elementary schools, Harrison Hill and Winding Ridge, having devoted themselves solely to inquiry-based learning. Project-based instruction is listed as the top curricular component in all of the elementary schools. There is also a charter school devoted to project-based learning called The Project School. Here, students are immersed in project-based learning linked to the state standards. Here are some of the methods they use for assessment (Project School, 2011):

- Literacy Assessments—conferences, interviews, anecdotal records, authentic student work, Reading Miscue Inventory
- Math/Logical Assessments—Investigations assessments, formal and informal teacher-created assessments, instructional rubrics
- P3 Ongoing Assessment—formal and informal teacher-created assessments, instructional rubrics
- Formal Standardized Assessments
- Student Exhibitions
- Museum of Authentic Work
- The Culminating Event
- Electronic Portfolios
- Student-Led Conferences
- Project School Progress Report
- Intensives (Assessment section)

There are schools out there basing their entire curriculums on project-based learning and finding great success. Ideally, you will be able to incorporate numerous disciplines into your projects. This multi-subject approach is more typical of what problems students will tackle in the real world, where issues are complex and must be addressed from a variety of vantage points.

INDIVIDUAL WORK VERSUS GROUP WORK

Some definitions of project-based learning specify that students must work in groups. Group work is not mandatory in PBL, but it has definite advantages. On the other hand, having students work individually allows them to develop something many gifted children struggle with: organization and responsibility. The student cannot depend on the teacher or group members in order to complete the project. Being organized might involve planning out activities on a calendar, setting expectations through the creation of a rubric, determining where to look for the content necessary for completing the project, and choosing what product best demonstrates learning.

A compromise between having students work individually and putting them into groups is assigning them partners. In this case, however, you must emphasize to students that this does not mean two people doing the work of one. Many times, what can happen with pairs is that students cut the work that an individual would do in half and split up the work. Part of the guidance you would provide as the teacher-coach would be to set expectations—namely, that the work would reflect that of two people, and maybe even more than that, given that the partners can help each other and work more efficiently.

Yet a third option is having students working in small groups. There are many advantages of gifted children working in collaborative group, including:

- the workload is divided;
- shy students are forced to interact with their peers;
- productivity may be increased, as students' progress affects others;
- different students' skillsets are combined;
- communication and cooperation are encouraged; and
- many students will one day hold jobs that require effective communication and interpersonal skills.

Students working in small groups are still given the many choices that project-based learning offers, but they must come to a consensus and compromise on these choices, given that there are multiple opinions to consider.

Some projects might lend themselves to a fourth option: having the entire class work as a group. A debate is an excellent example. Because a debate requires both an affirmative and a negative side, having two teams would be ideal. Rather than assigning specific roles, you could have the students decide who would fill the roles. They would conduct their own research and create the key points. They could debate subjects such as the use of stem cells, cloning, or whether the American colonists were justified in declaring independence from the British, or they could reenact the debate from *Inherit the Wind*. Other examples for whole-class activities include creating a class newspaper and involving students in an activity such as Math League, where they work out problems as a class.

Yet another option to consider is having students work as individuals, only to come together at the end of the project as a large group. This is known as a jigsaw approach. Each student works on a particular area that is part of a larger picture. Once students finish their own parts, they put those parts together with those of the other students, placing the pieces of the puzzle together to create one large picture.

An example of the jigsaw approach is a project covering the Impressionist movement. The movement could be broken down into several sections:

1. Japonisme: the French study of Japanese woodcut print art (ukiyo-e) introduced into French art circles. Examine this ancient art form and its strong influence on early Impressionist painters.
2. African mask art: Explore the influence of African culture and mask art on post-impressionism and early modern art. Examine mask art of tribes such as the Fang, BaTeke, and the BaKota and their influence on Picasso, Derain, Braque, Juan Gris, and Modigliani.
3. Early Impressionist painters: especially Monet and Manet. Define Impressionism and discuss its early influences. Other painters include Pissarro, Degas, Cassatt, Sisley, Renoir, Caillebotte, and Bazille.
4. Impressionist music: Research the influence of the Impressionist art style on the music of the times. Some musicians include Claude Debussy, Erik Alfred Satie, Cyril Scott, and Maurice Ravel.
5. Post Impressionist artists: How did art evolve after the Impressionist movement? Artists include Van Gogh, Gauguin, Seurat, Picasso, Rousseau, and Toulouse Lautrec, extending into the Early Modern and Expressionist periods.

6. Impressionist poetry: How did Impressionist art influence writing and poetry? Examine the writings of Paul Verlaine, Stephane Mallarme, Arthur Rimbaud, Charles Baudelaire, T. S. Eliot, e. e. cummings, and James Joyce.

In this project, each student would focus on an area of Impressionist art. Once the individual student had done his or her research and created an example of the art form, then he or she would sit down with the five students who covered the other areas; by putting all of the pieces together, students would see the overall influence, effect, and legacy of the Impressionist movement.

CURRICULUM-BASED VERSUS INQUIRY-BASED

The final area that can be adjusted is the source of the essential lesson that you want students to learn. Do you want the lesson to come directly from the state learning standard, or do you want students to generate the essential question themselves? Chapter 3 was all about using the state standards as the basis for projects in order to give students a focusing point. However, this does not mean that you have to let the standards limit the way the project is conducted. Take, for example, this fifth-grade science standard from the Ohio Department of Education (2002):

- Explain that Earth is one of several planets to orbit the sun, and that the moon orbits Earth. (p. 14)

If you are going to base the project exclusively on the state curriculum, you would break this down into two parts:

1. Explain that Earth is one of several planets to orbit the sun.
2. Explain that the moon orbits the Earth.

A student could create a project to research how the Earth orbits the sun, producing a model of the Earth using Styrofoam balls or maybe using classmates in a skit to reproduce the solar system, having students represent the various planets with signs indicating how long their orbits take. A similar project could be created to teach about the moon, perhaps incorporating how the gravity from the moon creates the tides or affects the fullness of the moon in the night sky. All students are working towards the same goal and will thoroughly understand the learning standards by the end of the project. The entire project would have taken place within the confines of the state curriculum, but would definitely qualify as PBL.

But consider an alternative scenario in which a teacher simply wrote two terms on the board:

The universe   The moon

The teacher would then allow 15 minutes for students to unpack what they knew about the two terms, writing their thoughts in a notebook. In this situation, there is no such thing as an incorrect thought. Students might think of things like The Beatles, who sang the song "Across the Universe," or they may write, "The cow jumped over it," referring to the nursery rhyme in which the cow jumps over the moon.

When the 15 minutes is up, students would share what they came up with, writing each idea on the board. It might look something like this:

```
        The universe              The moon

    Sun is center of the Milky Way

        stars                      Space travel
                    Earth  third  planet from sun

    Other planets have moons
                              Is Pluto a planet?
        Black holes        Neil Armstrong

                Takes 365 days to orbit Sun

    Life on  other planets?
                              Millions of universes
        Sun provides warmth
                                   Causes tides

                    Comets and asteroids
    Has a dark side
                    Many craters
                                   Nine planets

    Is it made of cheese?
```

The next step would be to cluster together these 18 topics into categories. The teacher would ask the class for suggestions on this. The clusters might look like this:

Earth third planet from Sun
Takes 365 days to orbit Sun

Space travel
Neil Armstrong

Has a dark side
Many craters
Is it made of cheese?
Causes tides
Stars
Black holes
Sun provides warmth

Sun is center of the Milky Way
Nine planets
Other planets have moons
Is Pluto a planet?

Life on other planets?
Millions of universes
Comets and asteroids

At this point, six topics exist. Students could choose which topics they would like to learn more about. Perhaps seven students would express interest for space travel, and only one person would be interested in stars. This is perfectly all right. The students would then research their topics and be responsible for teaching them to the class.

Notice that in this situation, everything that needed to be covered per the curriculum—the Earth orbiting the sun, the moon orbiting the Earth—is addressed. What is more, other material that interests students is also covered. This is why inquiry-based learning is so effective: Students are going beyond the bare minimum and branching out in other directions.

If, in this example, students did not address everything required by the curriculum (if, for instance, a student never mentioned the idea of the Earth taking 365 days to orbit the sun), you could suggest a topic to guide students. It is best, however, to let students do the driving, not realizing that they are covering the exact topics you set out for them to learn.

IN A NUTSHELL

There are many ways in which you can vary the structure of a project. You control whether projects:

- are teacher-led or student-led,
- happen sporadically or happen constantly,
- address only one subject or encompass many subject areas,
- are completed by individuals or are completed in groups, and
- are curriculum-based or based in inquiry.

You have the option of adjusting all of these variables, and you can adjust them throughout the project, finding the combinations that best fit your and your students' situation. Finding the right combination may take a series of trials and errors, but you should keep in mind that finding a single method and sticking with it is likely not the best option. You will want to allow yourself the flexibility to make adjustments when necessary.

6

Implementing the Structure With Students, Parents, Administration, and Staff

■ ■ ■ ■ ■ ■ ■ ■ ■ ■ ■ ■

INTRODUCTION

Now that you have used the last two chapters to determine the PBL structure that you will use, you have to make sure that your students understand it. As the teacher, you have the responsibility of giving students a clear enough understanding of the structure that they can work autonomously within it, also feeling empowered enough to work outside of it if necessary. This may be difficult, considering that most students, as well as their parents, are used to more traditional methods. This chapter will provide suggestions for how you might present the PBL structure.

TEACHING THE STRUCTURE TO STUDENTS

Once you have settled on a structure to try in the classroom, the teaching of that structure must be very purposeful. You cannot simply turn students loose on a project if they have never experienced PBL before and expect good results. Students have likely experienced classrooms in which the majority of information was provided for them and they simply had to comprehend—or at most, apply—what they were given. Students must be given permission and shown how to learn independently. Otherwise, they might fall into old patterns, and their work will remain at a lower level.

One way to model the process for students is through the use of a mini-project. This is a project designed to emulate what the structure of your actual project will look like, but it will take less time. If a project would usually take up to 5 weeks, you would compress this mini-lesson into 1 or 2 days. This gives the students a taste of what project structure will be like.

I did this with students when introducing the structure for my PBL science class. I explained the project structure that I had selected step by step, we went over how to use the calendar and rubric, and then I broke students up into groups and they conducted a mini-project that took only a single class period. This mini-project exposed them to the concepts of conducting research, pooling information, addressing essential learning goals, and creating a product. Students evaluated themselves and fellow students at the end of the class, and as group, we set the parameters for what an excellent product looked like, as well as defining a project that needed more improvement. Because this mini-lesson was not for a grade, students felt more comfortable taking risks, even if that meant failing. Several groups simply bit off more than they could chew and did not finish in time. We talked about how these teams could have managed their time differently to achieve success. Most students got the general idea of the project structure and set up from this mini-project and were then ready to try it on a much grander scale. An example mini-project called "Paper Versus Plastic" is included in Appendix B on page 104.

A second way to teach the structure to students is to run through the first full-length project as a class, holding the students' hands and walking them through the project step by step. You would create short-term, clear due dates that everyone would adhere to, and you would constantly remind students of these due dates. Students' products would all be due at the same time, although you might elect to allow students to choose their own products. (If your students could not handle that much responsibility, then you might want to assign all of your students the same product.)

Once this first project has been completed, you can determine whether the class is ready to strike out on its own. You may decide that some students are ready to strike out on their own, whereas other students still need more guidance. In this case, you can allow the first group to begin their independent projects while working more closely with the second group. This strategy allows you to ensure that all students understand the structure, and it serves to ease students from the traditional classroom into the PBL classroom.

You could also choose to introduce potential products at the beginning of the project, so that students could see the finish line before beginning the race. Because some students are so accustomed to taking pencil-and-paper tests upon completing a unit, they are often unsure of what to do when given free reign. You can begin by having a class discussion about various types of products that might be created. Although you may have a particular product in mind for students, you will often be surprised by what you get when you let them create for themselves.

I usually give students a wide range of products ideas, including the following:

- *Presentation:* Students get in front of the class and present what they have learned. Usually, students include a visual aid of some sort to guide their instruction. The details of the presentation come not in the text or in the visual aids, but in the verbal explanation. Presentation methods include PowerPoint, lecture, posters, and trifolds.
- *Exhibition:* Students report what they have learned in some visual form. This has to contain much more detailed text than a presentation would, because the only explanation of the learning comes from the item itself. Exhibition methods include models, posters, PowerPoint, and websites.
- *Portfolio:* This could refer either to a paper portfolio, wherein students collect articles and copies of websites or textbooks, or to a collection of websites whose addresses are pasted into a Word document. Students find materials that they learn

from, and then it is their responsibility to write up an explanation of what has been learned, with examples included.

- *Demonstration:* The student creates a hands-on experience for other students to participate in that teaches the learning outcomes. I had one student create a museum, and every exhibit in the museum had multiple demonstrations that taught the concept. The student acted as the museum guide, walking students from exhibit to exhibit and allowing them to participate in the demonstrations. Examples of demonstrations include experiments, models, and lessons.

- *Essay/Research Paper:* The student produces a formally written paper that answers the learning outcomes in text form. Spelling and grammar are weighted more heavily in this format.

- *Journal:* The student creates a daily journal of the time spent researching, also conducting some sort of long-term experiment and charting its daily progress. Journaling is less formal, so students are encouraged to explore their feelings and thoughts.

- *Test:* Students create their own tests to assess the learning outcomes. The format is similar to a state assessment, using multiple choice and constructed responses. The most important part of this product is the answer key. Students must provide detailed answers and rationale for these answers. If a test contains a multiple-choice question, the student who created that test must explain why the response listed in the answer key is correct.

- *Performance:* This category is, by design, completely open. Students are usually quite reluctant to choose this method at first, but as some brave students attempt a skit or song, others begin to try it as well. Soon this will become one of the more popular choices. I had one student who asked if he could make a video game. I told him that as long as the video game taught what it was supposed to, sure thing. He used free online video-game-making software to create a game following the quest of a knight to slay a dragon that taught students about physical and chemical changes. Examples of performance products include skits, video games, and songs.

If you need additional examples, I recommend a book called *The Ultimate Guide for Student Product Development and Evaluation* (2009), by Frances A. Karnes and Kristen R. Stephens.

To give students a better concept of products they might create, you might show them examples that you have collected over the years from your former students. This gives students tangible examples, and they can begin to envision for themselves what products they might make. I even went so far as to collect products that I had evaluated as excellent, good, and needs improvement so that students could see the differences among them.

Once students have seen what their products can look like, work backwards and discuss what sort of research would go into making such products and how this work could be planned out on a calendar.

Whichever of these strategies you use with your students, know that the process of teaching the PBL structure needs to be sound and deliberate if you expect to see your students thrive.

TEACHING STUDENTS HOW TO RESEARCH

Most PBL involves a research aspect. This research can take the form of books, Internet sources, interviews, and so on. Whichever form you want your students' research to take, you must be deliberate about teaching students how to research. You cannot assume that students already know how to do this, even if they are high school students. They might put up a good front of looking like they know how to conduct Internet searches, but you need to make sure that they know how to seek out substantive, not just stylish, sources.

You will want to take some time to ensure students understand how to research and what good research looks like. If you are primarily going to be using books, teach them the skills of using the table of contents, appendix, and index. If they are going to be conducting Internet research, go over with them which search engines are good ones, which ones to avoid, and how to synthesize that information into their own words. (An Internet Scavenger Hunt worksheet is included in Appendix A on pp. 95–96.) If students are going to be conducting interviews, teach them how to set up questions and yes, even how to make a phone call. In today's age of the cell phone, you might assume that students know how to talk on the phone, but there is a very large difference between how they talk to friends and how they should conduct a professional interview.

Note taking is a good skill to review with students. Being able to synthesize what information they have found into useful material for their projects is extremely valuable. I taught my third-grade gifted students how to take notes. It is a life-long, 21st-century skill that everyone can benefit from (see a sample note-taking lesson in Appendix B on pp. 123–127). You will also want to be sure to explain carefully and specifically what plagiarism is and is not and how students can put things into their own words, as well as how they should cite sources.

If you want to see good research, students have to see good research modeled first. If you teach students what good research looks like and how it is accomplished, the quality of their products will be greatly improved.

TEACHING THE STRUCTURE TO PARENTS

Almost as important as teaching the structure to the students is teaching it to their parents. Most parents of gifted kids like to be involved in the education of their children. If you begin implementing project-based learning without explaining it to parents, they might become confused about the expectations you have for their children, and in their frustration, they may paint the process as a negative one. If you explain your rationale for using PBL, then parents will often prove to be your greatest allies.

At the beginning of the year, I always hold a meeting with new parents to explain to them the philosophy and the processes of using project-based learning. In this meeting, I discuss the advantages to using PBL and what it will look like from their perspective when students bring home work that is unlike what the parents are used to seeing. I give parents suggestions for what they can do to help their children with PBL, such as going over research, taking them to the library to get resources, being an audience for their products, and so on. There are always lots of questions, and I answer each and every one of them in order to make sure that there is no confusion that could lead to miscommunication. I want to be sure that everything is clear.

In addition, I create a PowerPoint presentation that further explains the project structure and e-mail it to parents. This presentation provides a sample project so that parents can see for themselves what PBL might look like. Any communication with parents is good, but I have found that the more information I provide regarding PBL, the fewer questions and concerns come up later. You may want to be thorough in your explanation of PBL to parents when you embark upon project-based learning.

TEACHING THE STRUCTURE TO ADMINISTRATORS AND STAFF

Discussing PBL with your supervisor and principal is not only necessary, but also potentially beneficial, and talking about PBL with other teachers can be productive as well. Sometimes people scoff at what they don't understand, or they don't think that teaching methods are good for students if those methods don't look like those in other classrooms. Because project-based learning looks so different than the learning that occurs in the traditional classroom, it is important to make your principal aware of PBL's philosophies and how you intend to use it to raise the achievement level of your students. Letting administrators know ahead of time what your intentions are with this style of teaching will garner their support and prevent them from making assumptions. Make sure you point out that you are using the state standards as your core and will allow students to meet these standards at a higher level of learning. What principal wouldn't want to hear that?

You might also take the opportunity to inform your fellow teachers of your project-based learning approach. You could do this in a staff meeting, in a Critical Friends Group or some other professional learning community, or even in the staff lunchroom. Spread the word of PBL and its benefits. Others might be curious and willing to try it, and they might ask for guidance or suggestions. Some teachers might take elements of the PBL approach, such as rubrics or products, and incorporate them into their own classrooms. As teachers, we do not get to share best professional practices as often as we might like, so don't be afraid to share your own experiences with PBL.

IN A NUTSHELL

Setting up the structure so that students, parents, and administrators know how PBL works is beneficial for everybody. It will prevent you from having to answer hundreds of questions, and it will allow students to feel comfortable thinking outside the box. You will want to be clear with those involved and break the process down step by step, addressing how to begin, how to acquire content, and how to show what has been learned using products.

7

Teaching Students to Use Rubrics

■ ■ ■ ■ ■ ■ ■ ■ ■ ■ ■ ■ ■

INTRODUCTION

When you are setting up projects for students, as described in the last chapter, one way to offer the kind of choice that makes PBL more authentic is to give students the option of several products. A good way to evaluate these products is to use a rubric, but because the products students will make are so varied, you cannot have one template for grading them all. A presentation is going to be graded much differently than an electronic portfolio, and a research paper will be graded differently than those, and so on. You will need as many different rubrics as you have products. Some examples of rubrics that you may find helpful can be found in Appendix A. One approach is to use premade rubrics, such as those included in various books. You can also make your own rubrics using teacher websites such as RubiStar (http://rubistar.4teachers.org). Another method is to have students make their own rubrics. This is the option that I encourage and will discuss in this chapter.

EMPOWERING THE STUDENTS

Having the students create their own rubrics has many positive effects. Using self-made rubrics:

- clearly shows students how work is being evaluated,
- clarifies what the expectations of the project are,
- allows students to set high expectations for themselves, and
- acts as a motivational tool for students.

First and foremost, using self-made rubrics allows students to set their own expectations. Typically, students have expectations set for them by the teacher. As educators, we know that the level at which the bar is set for students is generally the level at which students will perform. Student-made rubrics allow them to set the bar, and thus, they may set it as high as they like. No one knows what a student is capable of better than the student. As the teacher, you might have to encourage some students to set the bar higher for themselves, especially underachieving gifted students, but more often than not, the students will expect more of themselves than the teacher does.

Another advantage to having students create their own rubrics is that this avoids a complaint often heard from students when they receive their grades: They have no idea how their teacher arrived at the mark. This is especially true regarding products for which grading is viewed as subjective, including essays and presentations. Because we are seeking higher level learning amongst our gifted students, there should be a certain level of openness to the learning outcome, making it somewhat subjective by nature. This subjectivity is the reason that having students create their own rubrics can be beneficial. This way, there is a clear blueprint for what students need to do in order to earn the highest grade, all planned out in the rubric. The student simply needs to have the rubric out while creating the product to know what to do. Also, if the student does not achieve the highest level of expectation, the teacher cannot be blamed, as the student was not only aware of the criteria, but created those criteria.

Yet another advantage of student-generated rubrics is that they empower students to be responsible for their education and learning—not only from the viewpoint of doing the work, but also from the viewpoint of how that work is evaluated. You can enhance this sense of empowerment by having students fill out self-evaluations. I always conference with students when handing back project grades, and the first question I ask is, "What grade do you think you deserved?" Nine times out of 10, the student either chooses an evaluation that is the same as my own, or in many cases, is tougher than I was. Very rarely does the student think his or her grade should have been higher than what I thought. When this does happen, a couple of follow-up questions generally help the student understand why the grade was not higher. It is very important for a student to be absolutely clear why his or her product received the grade it did. Otherwise, no learning will result from the experience. Rubrics go a long way towards making the grade clear and pointing out what aspects of performance could be improved next time.

THE FORMAT OF THE RUBRIC

A student-created rubric need not be very complex. In fact, as a rule of thumb, the simpler rubrics are, the better. This makes the rubric easier for the evaluator to grade and for the student receiving it to understand. Here is a basic template that can be modified to fit the needs of the assignment (a blank copy is included on p. 98 in Appendix A):

Student:_____ Project:_____

Excellent			
Good			
Needs Improvement			

In the first column, or the y-axis, you have the levels of assessment: excellent, good, and needs improvement. Depending on your purposes, these can be modified to reflect specific letter grades, specific number grades, or other categories. A word of caution: Too many categories can be confusing for both student and teacher. The x-axis has blanks where the students will create categories for how the product's evaluation is broken down, and each evaluation should include descriptions of each level. In this particular rubric, students have the opportunity to evaluate themselves on three levels. It is advisable to use at least this many levels so that students can easily identify where they need to work on something. If a rubric had only a single category, it would be difficult to offer specific feedback to be used for the following project. You could create more than three categories, but more than four or five start to get confusing for the grader. Remember, it's always best to keep it simple.

As the teacher, you might want to create your own category that will assess all projects. I always push responsibility with my projects, so I want to make sure students stay aware of that as they are working. As such, the blank rubric I provide them has this category already filled out:

Student:_____ Project:_____

				Responsibility/ Class Time
Excellent				1. Was on task for the majority of class time. 2. Made great use of exploration time, using the time given to find many learning opportunities. 3. Came to class fully prepared to work on the product with a plan in mind. 4. Turned in second evaluation with detailed comments.

Good				1. Was on task most of the time, but occasionally got off task.
				2. Made good use of exploration time, finding the basics.
				3. Came to class with what was needed for the product but not always with a plan.
				4. Turned in second evaluation but not detailed comments.
Needs Improvement				1. Was off task several times in class.
				2. Made poor use of exploration and was unfocused, finding little to no useful material.
				3. Came to class lacking what was needed for the product or didn't plan what to do.
				4. Did not turn in second evaluation.

You can see that in addition to ensuring that students remain on task and use class time wisely, this rubric requires each student to conduct a second evaluation for his or her product. This entails having a parent, another teacher, a fellow student, or even the student evaluating the product using the self-created rubric. In this way, I avoid seeing a rough draft of the product; somebody has evaluated the project and ideally has also provided suggestions for improvement. I provide students with extra copies of their rubrics, which they give to their second evaluators. These copies must be turned in with students' final products.

TEACHING STUDENTS HOW TO MAKE THE RUBRIC

As with most aspects of project-based learning, when it comes to rubrics, the groundwork you lay in the beginning will make things that much easier down the road. You cannot just give students a blank rubric and expect them to know how to create it. This must be taught. The teaching of how to create a rubric can be broken down into four steps:

- Step 1: Create categories.
- Step 2: Provide descriptions of each category.
- Step 3: Have a tiered system for the descriptions.
- Step 4: Check the rubric over.

The first of these steps is to create categories. This is simply breaking the product down into smaller, more manageable parts. There are times when students will do one part of the project very well, and yet falter in another aspect. For example, a student might have had excellent information and research, but a wooden presentation. You want to give credit for the job well done on content, yet point out what the student needs in order to improve future presentations. If the student received a single overall grade, it might be difficult to see what could be improved and what had been achieved.

Students should break down their products into categories that make sense. Here is an example of a rubric that has broken down a presentation:

	Content	Organization	Presentation
Excellent			
Good			
Needs Improvement			

The student has created three logical categories: the content, which is the meat of the product; the actual presentation; and a third category, organization, which can be an issue when presenting. Another possibility for a category may have been PowerPoint, if that was the method the student used to present, or even professionalism, which would cover such aspects as how the visual aid looked and the student's conduct.

One category that would probably not fit very well is spelling and grammar, as those skills are not as prominent or as important in a presentation as they are in, say, an essay. Even a category like visuals would likely be too narrow and would not cover all of the aspects of a PowerPoint presentation. Coming up with categories can sometimes be difficult for students, especially those who see only the big picture. You may have to assist them and suggest categories at first, but after a while, students will get the hang of breaking the product down into parts, a skill that will improve their organization and analytical abilities.

Once the categories have been set, the second step is to create a description for how those categories will be evaluated. When doing this, it is a good idea to start with the top level, which in the example is an excellent. The reason for doing this is twofold; first, it establishes the top, from which the middle and bottom levels can be formed, and second, it teaches students to start with the best, so that the highest level of achievement is viewed as the baseline or the expectation.

The description should be a sentence or two and should show how the category would look if achieved. The more vague the description is, the more difficult it will be to evaluate. Lots of students want to start with the following description:

The content is excellent.

The problem with this description is that what is excellent to one person might not qualify as excellent to another. A student might think the content is excellent if one example is included. A teacher might think three examples make for excellent content. The more specific the description is, the more objective the grading of the product can be.

This leads us back to our initial question: What does excellent content look like? This can be broken down much like the product itself was broken down. It is a good idea to have at least three descriptions for each level of the category. This is enough of a breakdown to make the category objective, but not so broken down that it becomes confusing to grade. I have had students use four or five descriptions, but that is pushing it a little.

Let's say the student has broken the content down into three descriptive words:

- Detail
- Examples
- Depth

You cannot just list these in the category of excellent content. Once again, to do this would be too vague and subjective. The students need to show what excellent content really looks like. Thus, the above words can be fleshed out into the following:

- Has lots of *details* that help explain and make clear the learning outcome.
- Gives lots of *examples* that add to the understanding of the learning outcome.
- Goes into *depth* on what the learning outcome is, teaching more than is required.

It is clear now what content looks like at an excellent level to both the teacher and the student. A student knows what he or she has to provide, and the teacher knows how to grade it.

With our three descriptions, this is what the rubric looks like now:

	Content	Organization	Presentation
Excellent	1. Has lots of details that help explain and make clear the learning outcome. 2. Gives lots of examples that add to the understanding of the learning outcome. 3. Goes into depth on what the learning outcome is, teaching more than is required.		
Good			
Needs Improvement			

Once you have created 3–5 descriptions in the top category, the next step is creating descriptions for the middle and lower categories. This is known as a tiered system. Whatever you put in the top category also has to be reflected in the subsequent categories. So our three key words—detail, examples, and depth—must also be addressed at the good and needs improvement levels in our example rubric. It is helpful to have the students number their descriptions so they are easier to keep track of. So in the excellent description, we had:

- Has lots of details that help explain and make clear the learning outcome.

That means that in the good category, we will label the descriptions about details as 1 to correspond to the number 1 in the excellent category, with the same being true for the details description in the needs improvement category. The examples description will get the number 2 in all three levels, and the depth of content descriptions will all be numbered 3.

When making the descriptions for the lower levels, the good news is that you do not have to completely rewrite the description; you simply need to alter it. The easiest way of doing this is to alter the description using the word *but* for the middle category and the word *not* for the lowest category. For example, the description in the good section for detail would look like this:

- Has many details that help explain and make clear the learning outcome, *but* is missing a few where needed.

With the addition of a few choice words, the description has gone from excellent to good.

Similarly, with the needs improvement level, adding the word *not* can change the meaning of the description appropriately:

- *Does not* have a lot of detail that helps explain and make clear the learning outcome.

You would do this for the other two descriptions in the excellent tier as well, using *but* and *not* to change their meanings, such as in the example that follows:

	Content	Organization	Presentation
Excellent	1. Has lots of details that help explain and make clear the learning outcome. 2. Gives lots of examples that add to the understanding of the learning outcome. 3. Goes in depth on what the learning outcome is, teaching more than is required.		

	Content		
Good	1. Has many details that help explain and make clear the learning outcome, but is missing some where needed. 2. Gives a lot of examples that add to the understanding, but more are needed in places. 3. Goes into depth in places, but other times teaches just what was required.		
Needs Improvement	1. Does not have a lot of detail, and learning outcomes are unclear. 2. Does not give a lot of examples. 3. Does not go into depth, sometimes not even teaching what was required.		

Once students have completed descriptions for the first category, they will need to repeat steps two and three for the other two categories until completing the rubric:

	Content	Organization	Presentation
Excellent	1. Has lots of details that help explain and make clear the learning outcome. 2. Gives lots of examples that add to the understanding of the learning outcome. 3. Goes in depth on what the learning outcome is, teaching more than is required.	1. Has lots of slides (5–7) per objective. 2. Has one visual per slide that explains learning outcome clearly. 3. Clearly states which learning outcome is being addressed so that it is easy for the audience to follow.	1. Speaks loudly enough that everyone in the audience can hear. 2. Seems to know the material and can answer all questions. 3. Presents the PowerPoint, rather than reading the slides.

Good	1. Has many details that help explain and make clear the learning outcome, but is missing some where needed. 2. Gives a lot of examples that add to understanding, but more are needed in places. 3. Goes into depth in places, but other times teaches just what was required.	1. Has a sufficient number of slides (3-4) per objective. 2. Has lots of good visuals, but not one on every slide. 3. States which learning outcome is being addressed sometimes, but not always, leading to a little confusion.	1. Speaks loudly enough for people to hear, but sometimes mumbles or is hard to understand. 2. Seems to know the material most of the time, but struggles with a question or two. 3. Presents rather than reading the slides most of the time, but reads at times.
Needs Improvement	1. Does not have a lot of detail, and learning outcomes are unclear. 2. Does not give a lot of examples. 3. Does not go into depth, sometimes not even teaching what was required.	1. Does not have many slides (1-2) per objective. 2. Has very few visuals or does not explain the learning outcome. 3. Very rarely or never states which learning outcome is being addressed, leading to confusion.	1. Does not speak loudly enough and is difficult to hear at times. 2. Does not seem to know the material and has great difficulty with questions. 3. Reads the slides more than presenting them.

Step 4 of this process requires the student to look over the rubric to make sure that it has met all of the requirements. The student will want to check that the rubric:

- contains at least three categories, with at least three descriptions in each;
- has the same number of descriptions in each category;
- is legible for the evaluator to use; and
- has descriptions that fit the categories (e.g., content description should not be in the organization category, visual description should not be in the speaking category).

Once the student has checked over the rubric, it needs to be approved by the teacher.

TEACHER APPROVAL OF THE RUBRIC

You will need to evaluate the rubric and make sure that it is where it needs to be. Ultimately, you will be the one using these rubrics to evaluate your students. You want to make sure that you are able to use them effectively and as the student intended. I conference individually with every student, checking over his or her rubric, and most of the time, I require some sort of revision. Here are some common issues to look for in students' rubrics:

- The excellent descriptions should push the students to an excellent level.
  - o Students will sometimes have very low expectations of the project or will not realize what it means to be excellent. Especially with gifted students, the bar should be placed fairly high and might be placed higher for one student than it will be for another.
- The good or middle level should be just that: good.
  - o Describing the top and the bottom levels seems to be easy for students. It is finding that middle level that is tricky for them. Check that their descriptions for this category indeed describe good products and are not too lax.
- Students should avoid descriptions that measure meaningless skills.
  - o While searching for three categories, students will sometimes get desperate and evaluate something that is not all that important. For instance, under spelling/grammar, a student might have the description "Uses correct capitalization." If you are dealing with older students who should already have this skill, or if it is a math project, then this skill might not be important enough to warrant a description. A better choice for a description might have something to do with proper sentence structure, or you might suggest an entirely different category.
- Make sure that descriptions are specific and not vague.
  - o Students often use the word "some," as in, "There are some examples." The problem is that the word some is very subjective. One is some, and 100 is some, but they are very different numbers. Have students use more specific descriptions, like many or few.
- Students should have some flexibility in their descriptions and should not be too extreme.
  - o In the needs improvement level of the evaluating spelling criterion, students may write, "Spelling is not correct." It is unlikely that a student would misspell every single word, and if there are some correctly spelled words, the student could argue that this description did not apply to the product, even if it contained many misspelled words. This description is too extreme. A better description would be "Contains many spelling mistakes"—if possible, even more specific than that.
- Descriptions should be concrete when possible.
  - o Students are prone to creating descriptions like, "Has many slides in Power-Point presentation." What constitutes the term "many" is subjective. The student might think that 10 would constitute many, while the teacher might think 20 would. Have students measure whenever possible. "Has 20 slides in Power-Point presentation" is much more specific and easy to measure.
- The levels are balanced and match up.

o Students may put in the excellent level, "Has 20 slides in PowerPoint presentation," and then put in the good level, "Has 15 slides in PowerPoint presentation." What happens if there are 17 slides? A better system would contain descriptions such as, "Has 20 slides in PowerPoint presentation" in the excellent level, "Has 15–19 slides in PowerPoint presentation" in the good level, and "Has 14 and below slides in PowerPoint presentation" in the needs improvement level.

- Descriptions should not be used multiple times.
    o A student will sometimes repeat a description in two categories. One problem with this is that if the student does not succeed, the product is penalized twice. Each skill should be evaluated only once. If you want to give more weight to a certain skill, then you can reflect that in the rubric with weighted categories.
- When considered overall, the rubric will accurately evaluate the project as a whole.
    o If the product is a presentation, does the rubric successfully evaluate the relevant aspects of a presentation, or are important aspects overlooked? Be sure that a rubric is not too broad or too narrow.

Just like the students, you will get more comfortable with rubrics, and better at evaluating which rubrics work and which do not, especially once you start using them to grade. It is important to be diligent and have students make the necessary corrections and revise the rubrics themselves in order for them to learn.

GRADING WITH A RUBRIC

When you grade students' products, you look for detail and examples that help demonstrate the student's knowledge and communicate the point effectively. Similarly, *you* need to provide detail and examples when grading using a rubric in order for students to see what they need to improve upon. If you simply circle a description without providing any comments, the student might not understand where the shortcoming occurred. It is often difficult to provide a lot of detail regarding a presentation, where you are grading in real time and things move on as you are writing something down. You must do your best knowing that the more detailed you can be, the more clear your feedback will be to the student.

There are different approaches to take when grading with a rubric. Some people make notes on a separate piece of paper or on the back of the rubric as they are going along:

> Objective 1
> - Model was realistic
> - Explained objective well
> - Did a fairly good job explaining the 3 sources
>   of power for future city.
> - Types of power sources in current cities
>   explained along w/benefits & drawbacks for each
>
> Objective 2
> - Somewhat organized. Needs to speak a little
>   more clearly.
> - Could use a few more examples.
> - Could flow a little more smoothly
> - Learned about "micro" and "pico" dams - Good
>   explanations
>
> Objective 3
> - Need to tie in "future power" w/ future city

When finished, they simply evaluate the rubric using the notes taken. The advantage of this approach is that it allows for lots of detail and examples to be recorded. The disadvantage is that going back and forth between the notes and the rubric might cause something to be lost or overlooked, and doing this is sometimes quite time consuming.

Another approach is to make the notes right on the rubric itself. The teacher circles the appropriate description and makes a comment next to it. For every circle that is made, there is a comment accompanying it, so that students know what they did well and what they need to work on. This is what a rubric completed in this fashion looks like:

	Content	Visuals	Presentation	Responsibility/Class Time
Excellent (E)	1. Covers whats needed and goes further. 2. Provides most facts with examples 3. Goes into detail on all obj's	1. Has a visual on every slide. 2. Makes continuous references to the pictures. 3. Visual fits what's being explained, and helps with the explanation.	1. Speakers speak clearly and confidently. 2. Presentation is delivered professionally, staying on task 3. Has 25+ slides	1. Was on task a majority of class time. 2. Made great use of exploration time, using the time given to find many learning opportunities. 3. Came to class fully prepared to work on product with a plan in mind. 4. Turned in 2nd evaluation with detailed comments
Good (M-P)	1. Covers what's needed but not further. 2. Provides some facts with examples but not... 3. Goes into some detail on all obj's, but could be more	1. Has a visual on almost every slide but not every. 2. Makes occasional references to visuals but structures... 3. Visual usually fits what's being explained, but sometimes is there for no apparent reason.	1. Speaks... but not... 2. ... 3. Has 15-24 slides	1. Was on task most times but occasionally got off task. 2. Made good use of exploration time, finding the basics. 3. Came to class with what was needed for the product but not always with a plan. 4. Turned in 2nd evaluation but not detailed comments
Needs Improvement (L)	1. Does not cover what is needed 2. Does not provide facts with examples. 3. Does not go into detail on any obj's	1. Has few visuals. 2. Doesn't make references to visuals. 3. Most pictures don't fit in and are out of place.	1. Speaker does not speak clearly, confidently. 2. Presentation is not delivered professionally, off topic 3. Less than 15 slides.	1. Was off task several times in class. 2. Made poor use of exploration time, mostly fumbled around finding nothing. 3. Came to class lacking what was needed for the product or didn't plan what to do. 4. Did not turn in 2nd evaluation

The advantage here is that the comments are tied directly to the descriptions on the rubric. Students know exactly what they did well and why, as well as what they need to work on. The disadvantage, as you can see, is that this sort of feedback tends to be scattered and could be confusing or overwhelming.

Whichever approach you take, I strongly suggest that rather than simply passing back the graded rubrics to students as you would a worksheet or another graded paper, you should sit down and conference with the students individually about the comments you made on their rubrics and how your reached the evaluation you did. This way, you can be sure that students are clear on matters, and they will be less likely to repeat the same mistakes after having them pointed out twice—once on the rubric, and another time verbally. This is an important part of the coaching element of PBL, the topic of Chapter 9.

IN A NUTSHELL

Teaching your students to create their own rubrics can be a huge advantage in a project-based learning classroom, especially if you have multiple choices for the products that students can create. In addition, making their own rubrics empowers students to be more aware of the expectations of a project, because they are the ones who set those expectations.

It is important to teach students how to create rubrics properly. Having a clear method and structure go a long way towards making this process easier. Remember to check over students' rubrics and have them make revisions so that you can use the rubrics easily and effectively. A good rubric:

- is simple;
- is easy to use;

- justifies your evaluation clearly for the student;
- contains categories which, when considered together, offer a fair holistic representation of a project; and
- does not evaluate skills irrelevant to the class, project, or product.

8

Technology, Resources, and Classroom Environment

■ ■ ■ ■ ■ ■ ■ ■ ■ ■ ■ ■ ■ ■

INTRODUCTION

If someone were to walk into a project-based learning classroom, it would look very different than what people are used to seeing in a traditional setting. Students would be scattered about, each working on something different. While one might be writing a paper, another might be painting a model of the universe, while yet another might be creating a trifold with pictures. Someone else might be on the phone conducting an interview, and another person might have headphones on and be watching an online video. The PBL classroom can best be described as organized chaos.

Because each student's work is so different, the classroom needs to be set up differently as well. Having students sitting in perfectly lined up rows, all facing the front of the room, is fine if the teacher is going to be lecturing or giving instruction for a majority of the time, but this setup is quite restrictive in the project-based learning classroom. During one of my first years teaching, I shared a room with another teacher. In my class, students often worked in groups, so we would move the seats around to facilitate group work. The other teacher got so tired of my students messing up his rows that he placed tape on the floor to show how the desks needed to be rearranged. PBL is going to be difficult for you if you are a tape-on-the-floor sort of teacher. This chapter will give you suggestions and tips for how to set up your classroom.

THINK OF THE CLASSROOM AS AN OFFICE

When students go to school, they are essentially going to work. School is their job for the first 18 years of their lives. The question to ask yourself when setting up your classroom is, "Do students have everything they need in this classroom in order to be successful at their job?" If you were an artist, you would need a studio with paints and a canvas. If you were a realtor, you would need an office with a phone, a fax machine, and a parking space. If you were a scientist, you would need a lab with test tubes, various chemicals, and a sink. So what do students involved in project-based learning need?

This, of course, depends on the project. If students were charged with creating a trifold, they would need markers, pencils, rulers, and other art supplies. If they chose to create a PowerPoint presentation, they would need Microsoft Office and Internet access to find visuals. There are several things to consider when setting up your PBL classroom.

TECHNOLOGY IN THE CLASSROOM

When I began teaching 15 years ago, the most technological advance we learned about in my university teacher training was the overhead projector. Technology has come a long way since then. Now students can create their own websites and download podcasts to the Internet for the world to hear.

Some schools have lots of technology, and others have very little. The importance of using technology in the classroom is very high, especially in the 21st century. More and more, technology is vital in the workforce across a broad range of spectrums—across salary ranges, in public and private sectors, and in nearly every area. The more often students use technology, the better prepared they will be to live in a world where technology is dominant.

Of course, some students will demonstrate technological know-how that will leave you flabbergasted, and this is particularly true for gifted students. I have had students who were directors of their own films and wanted to incorporate these skills into as many projects as possible. Other students had the ability to write code to create their own websites. One student created an interactive PowerPoint that modeled the popular game show *Who Wants to Be a Millionaire?* (including the tense theme music), while others used MovieMaker to narrate their own documentaries. The possibilities are endless, but students cannot demonstrate their skills unless they are given opportunities.

Teaching your students basic technology skills is a valuable endeavor to undertake. I've had many a teacher scoff at me for showing my third graders how to create a PowerPoint, or a parent who could not believe that her child had to write a formatted research paper at so young an age. You can never introduce technology too early to a child. Because there is so much to learn in regard to technology, the younger children are when they begin to learn, the more time they have to master the technology. Because there is more opportunity for one-on-one coaching in PBL, you can actually sit down with a student and demonstrate how to add slides to a PowerPoint, or encourage the student to film a commercial that teaches the concept. You can meet each student where he or she is in regard to knowledge of technology and extend students' boundaries.

You can also learn from students. Don't be afraid to ask a student how something was created, or if you could borrow an idea or two. You can also take advantage of the free seminars often provided for educators. Because technology is constantly advancing, it is important to stay up to date on your own skills. When I began teaching, my mother—who had taught for 30 years—told me always to befriend the school's administrative assistants and custodians, as being friendly with them makes a teacher's job much easier. In the 21st century, I would expand my mother's advice to include being friendly with the technology trainer in your district. In addition to the fact that they are typically very nice people, it's very useful to have a friend who knows what to do when your technology breaks down or you need something downloaded quickly, and people are always more likely to help a friend than they are an unfamiliar face.

It is very important for students to have access to computers, although this obviously depends on your situation. With the Internet, your students can explore endless avenues of research for free. You will have to teach your students how to navigate through all of the junk out there in order to conduct an effective search, but once they learn that skill, the information they can gather is unlimited. For the last few years, I have had the advantage of having a laptop cart in my classroom so that every student has his or her own computer with Internet access. Originally, we had four classroom desktops, and I had to come up with a system where students rotated every 15 minutes or so. I also made liberal use of the computer lab, signing up to use it whenever possible to give my students access to technology. Don't be shy about hogging the computer lab. What I have found is that many people do not take advantage of it. The laptop cart I currently use was sitting in a back room and hadn't been used for a couple of years. Take advantage of the technology your district offers. Also, don't hesitate to ask around. You would be surprised what you can get if you just ask. When I started teaching, I badly wanted a laptop to use in the classroom so that I could show students PowerPoint presentations for some of my social studies topics. I went to my building principal and asked him for a laptop. He looked at me carefully for a moment, and then he nodded his head. One week later, I had a brand-new laptop and was using it in my classroom. Other teachers asked me a bit jealously why I had received a laptop when they had been working at the school longer than I had and still had not been given laptops. Whenever I asked these teachers whether they had asked for laptops, they seemed surprised—none of them had asked. The worst possible response you can get if you ask for something is "No." That's all—no public floggings or abject humiliation.

Some other suggestions for technology that can be valuable in a PBL classroom are:

- **Flip camera:** This is a fairly simple camera that even the most technologically naïve student can operate. It is about the size of a tape recorder and has simple buttons. It is easy to download the video to a computer simply by plugging it in and making a transfer, and then students can manipulate it however they like.
- **LCD projector:** This device attaches to a computer and can project the image from the computer screen. This is valuable in several ways. When students present a PowerPoint, for instance, you want the entire class to see it. Or you may have an interesting website or online video to share with students. A cheaper alternative would be to have an overhead projector that students could use to project images.
- **Interactive whiteboard:** Here, the computer image is projected on the whiteboard, and then the teacher or students can manipulate the image by touching the board. If your goal is merely to project, then a simple screen will work just as well, if not better. Use this piece of technology only if you have planned a presentation with hands-on components.
- **Teacher webpage:** Having a webpage where parents and students can access information is always a plus. Although it takes a little time to create and maintain, it prevents lots of questions that would probably take up even more of your time. I have a webpage that lists project descriptions and has blank calendars and rubrics that students can print out. This way if a student is absent for a few days, there is no excuse not to have kept up with work. The website also helps parents to understand how the projects work.

- **Telephone:** Most classrooms are equipped with a teacher phone. Make this phone available to students. (Of course, you will probably want to monitor them as they are using the phone.) Have phonebooks and directories for the local universities so that students can call experts for interviews. You would be amazed how willing people are to talk to students. One of my students called a professor at The Ohio State University concerning her rock project and actually set up a face-to-face interview at his office. Later on in the year, we were watching the Academy Award-winning documentary *An Inconvenient Truth*, and a world-renowned expert on geology was discussing ice samples from the Arctic. My student said, "Hey, that's the guy I interviewed for my rock project."

Conversely, though, is important not to rely too heavily on technology in the PBL classroom. If a student can create a more effective visual aid with markers and poster board than with a drawing tableau program, then that is the better option. If using the interactive whiteboard actually stymies the presentation rather than enhancing it, then a more traditional method should be used. Students often want to add sound effects and visuals to PowerPoints that do not teach anything, but rather distract the audience. Many people think that simply using technology improves a project. Technology is like any tool; it has to be used properly in order to garner positive results. Sometimes technology can even slow down the education process and make students focus more on the technology than on what they are supposed to be learning. Make sure that students understand when, where, and how these tools should be used by showing them examples of past student products. It is important for you to keep students focused on the big picture of the learning outcome.

OTHER RESOURCES

Technology is not a necessity in the PBL classroom, although it is extremely helpful. There are other ways for students to produce their products. Some students who are not fans of technology may be quite talented at performing skits, creating models with clay, or designing posters, which can be as or even more effective than creating similar products with technology.

Because students have so many choices in PBL, they need just as many choices when it comes to resources. In some cases, students may provide consumables such as trifolds, poster boards, model magic clay, and other similar products, but as the teacher, you can supply the tools needed to create on these canvases. Items that would be good to keep in the classroom might include:

- markers, crayons, colored pencils, and paint;
- glue and tape;
- construction paper, printer paper, and magazines; and
- rulers, yardsticks, and compasses.

These are fairly inexpensive materials that will allow your students to create their products without having to cart things back and forth from home. I even keep a small tool box in the closet of my classroom that contains a hammer, screwdrivers, and various other tools. It has come in handy more than a few times with student projects.

Another easy resource to provide for students is a collection of books concerning the topic they are studying. Most public libraries, and even some school libraries, keep a good variety of educational books that can be checked out and kept in the classroom. If you know your students are going to be learning about the ancient Romans, then go to the library and pick up a dozen or so books on the subject. These do not need to be the thick, scholarly books, either. Eyewitness Books, Smithsonian Handbooks, Expert Guides, and other such series aimed at students are great resources, even for high school students. These books do an excellent job of breaking down large topics into simple sections and explaining things in a clear way. I usually have students begin with these books before moving on to the Internet, because the books provide a basic overview.

Another cheap and effective resource is having experts come into your classroom and talk to students, either one on one or to the group. Being able to talk to another human being and ask questions directly are extremely valuable skills, students will remember information that they gather in this fashion far better than they will from reading it in a book or seeing it on the Internet. An easy place to start in terms of finding experts is your students' parents. Have them come in and give mini-lessons or offer advice to students, or find expert mentors that students can call for advice, guidance, and information. During a creative writing project that my students did, each student kept in contact with a professional writer through e-mail or by phone. With their mentors, students could brainstorm ideas, have their mentors look at various drafts, and be ask questions when they got stuck. Plus, students got the sort of individualized attention that is sometimes hard to provide when you have a classroom full of 30 students. With the Internet and the inexpensive cost of cell phones, the experts need not even be local. You could have your student conferring with people from countries halfway across the world.

Teachers often forget one valuable resource: themselves. You are a valuable resource as well, and you need to make yourself available to students. Because of the way the traditional classroom is set up, oftentimes students think of the teacher as the purveyor of rules and regulations rather than as a person who has something to offer. You need to cultivate an atmosphere in which students know that they can come to you for advice and guidance, just as they would consult a textbook or an Internet site. This means that you should make yourself available to them when they are working, rather than grading papers or sitting at your desk in the corner. Walk around and offer advice to students when you see they are stuck, or show them a cool website they can use in their research or an interesting way to set up their product. Once students begin to realize that you are there as a resource, they will be more likely to use you in that capacity.

CREATING THE AMBIANCE

For those of you who have always had your own classrooms, the joy of having a classroom may be difficult to understand—but as someone who spent his first 2 years teaching from a cart, I still consider having a classroom a privilege. Having a classroom is a great advantage and should be used as such. The way you set up your classroom will immediately set the tone for how students should act in your classroom. If you have the desks all lined up in perfect rows, and if everything posted around the classroom is about following rules, then students will come in and give you that same type of linear thinking. If, however, your room is colorful and set up in a unique fashion, then that is the type of thinking you will get from students—colorful and unique.

Something as simple as throwing a couple of bean bag seats in a corner or bringing in an old couch can do wonders for creating the more relaxed atmosphere that is conducive to PBL. If possible, you should have students sitting at tables rather than at desks, giving them the ability to move things around whenever necessary. As the teacher, you will have to be flexible with PBL, trying different methods of teaching and learning to find the correct fit. Likewise, your students will have to be flexible in learning how to think outside the box. Your classroom will need to be flexible, as well. If students are working in groups, they will need to position their chairs to be able to work together better. If you want to have a discussion, you should be able to move the chairs into a circle to facilitate interaction. If you are having a guest speaker come in, the chairs will need to be lined up facing the front so that students can pay attention properly.

Another thing you can do very easily to create the proper ambiance in your classroom environment is to use music. Playing music can set a more relaxed tone and allow students to open up their minds a bit more. Brewer (2008) cited many advantages of using music in the classroom in her book *Soundtracks for Learning: Using Music in the Classroom.*

Benefits of Music Use in Daily Life	**Classroom Outcomes of Music Use**
♪ Do you ever play music because it makes you feel happy and more eager to do what you need to do?	Play music to set a positive mood at the start of the day or at the beginning of a class. Play music throughout the day during breaks and transitions to maintain a positive attitude.
♪ Do you play music to energize yourself when you first wake up or feel tired?	Raise student energy levels with upbeat music as needed throughout the day.
♪ Have you found that music can calm and soothe you or your family members?	Play music to reduce stress levels, relieve frustration, and create a peaceful classroom environment.
♪ Does music sometimes help you focus on the task at hand?	Use music to help sustain student attention and concentration.
♪ Do you find that music can inspire you, motivate you, and build your enthusiasm?	Play music to motivate and inspire your students.
♪ Do you use music to help get things done more quickly and easily?	Play music during independent work and group activities.
♪ Does music stimulate your creativity?	Use music during writing, arts projects, and reflective activities.
♪ Does certain music bring back memories and the emotional experience of an event?	During learning activities, play music that will create an appropriate emotional connection to the information and provide a trigger for recall.
♪ Does music help you relax and reflect on issues and ideas?	Play slow, quiet music while you calmly review lesson information for students.

♪ Does music help you connect to and cooperate with others?	Play music to encourage interaction and build classroom community.
♪ Do you play music for fun?	Use music in the classroom to increase the joy of learning.

From *Soundtracks for Learning: Using Music in the Classroom* (p. 3), by C. B. Brewer, 2008, Bellingham, WA: Lifesounds Educational Services. Copyright © 2008 by Lifesounds Educational Services. Reprinted with permission.

I usually prefer to use music without lyrics, such as classical pieces or movie soundtracks, so that the music acts as a background instead of distracting students. Occasionally I will choose music that fits the project, such as songs from the 80s when students are creating timelines based on the Billy Joel song "We Didn't Start the Fire," or music from a culture we are studying (e.g., Aboriginal music, Native American music, Mesoamerican music). I even play music during assessments, and I find that it blocks out a lot of the distracting, extraneous noise usually audible during silence, such as tapping pencils, coughs, and sounds from outside that are magnified in a completely quiet classroom.

IN A NUTSHELL

If you don't want your project-based classroom to run like a traditional classroom, then it cannot look like a traditional classroom. The flexibility of PBL needs to be reflected in your classroom setup, from the furniture arrangement to the resources available to students.

Having access to technology will allow your students a lot of flexibility, creating products even you hadn't considered. If your district does not have much technology, or if you wish to provide other resources, consider library books, guest experts, and yourself. Even something as simple as setting the mood with music can go a long way towards creating the PBL environment.

9

Teaching in the Project-Based Classroom: Becoming a Coach

INTRODUCTION

The role of the teacher in a project-based learning classroom is much different from the role of the teacher in the traditional classroom. In a traditional classroom, the teacher is the source of all knowledge and controls everything that goes on, from the day-to-day schedule to the student activities. In a PBL classroom, the source of all knowledge is the students. It is they who determine the activities and how the schedule will run, as dictated by the project needs.

Because of this, the teacher no longer stands in front of the class as the focal point. Instead, he or she will blend into the classroom, becoming just another part of the whole. If you are used to doing a lot of talking in the classroom, you may view this as an unimportant or diminished role. In fact, the role of the PBL teacher is just as important as the role of the traditional teacher, if not more important.

WHAT COACHING LOOKS LIKE

Once you find the correct structure for your classroom and have your students working independently, the question becomes what *you* are supposed to do while students are working. Students are working autonomously on their projects, and they know where to get their resources and how to use them, so what part do you play in this PBL world?

The role of the teacher is more that of a coach. A coach does not run plays or execute plans. Sure, a coach sets up schemes and structures, but most of the coach's time once the season begins is spent on the sidelines, hoping the players are able to live up to the potential of their talent. As a coach, you are the organizer, but the players do most of the actual work. The same goes for your students in a PBL environment; they are doing most of the work, which is how learning should be.

There are many benefits to this approach of coaching in the classroom. According to Stix and Hrbek (2006), coaching in the classroom:

- improves classroom morale and motivation,
- enhances an interactive environment,
- increases the ability to resolve conflicts,
- encourages better organization,
- promotes creativity and high-level scholarship,
- lowers students' stress levels, and
- increases student productivity.

In the classroom, this coaching of your students takes the form of:

- managing stress of students learning the new strategies of PBL;
- giving students space to make mistakes;
- keeping students focused on the learning objectives and preventing them from getting too caught up in the product;
- conferencing with students to make sure they are on the right track, figuring things out, and growing as learners; and
- intervening with groups only when it seems that students are not going to be able to create a resolution on their own.

A good coach is careful about dispensing information and knows when to step in and when to stay out of the way. Maintaining this balance is now your job as the teacher in a PBL classroom. Finding this balance is the tricky part.

MANAGING STRESS

Any change to the typical classroom environment can be very stressful for students—especially gifted students, who often prefer routine. Because project-based learning is so different from what students have done before, this change can lead to stress. As the coach, you have to be conscious of students' stress and do what you can to alleviate it.

One strategy you can consider to manage stress is to introduce project-based learning slowly, rather than throwing the students in the pool before they know how to swim. Moving students from traditional styles of learning to exclusively project-based learning can be compared to taking an animal out of its regular ecosystem and plopping in into a totally different one. Some animals may adapt right away, but others will struggle to survive. Much as a nature preserve eases an animal into the wild, you might ease students into the PBL environment, especially if you get the sense that you have students who might be shell shocked by so many changes. Introduce projects within a traditional setting so that students are not completely immersed in it. Intermingle traditional classroom techniques such as lectures and worksheets throughout a project. Once students seem as though they are getting more comfortable with it, you can wean them off of the traditional methods, if you so choose, and transition to complete PBL.

Another strategy to consider is to spend the first month of school preparing students for PBL. I do this with my students, waiting to begin any projects until I have had sufficient time to have them enter the waters and get used to the temperature before asking them to swim. For instance, when I worked with elementary school students, I used a bubble gum unit that introduced them to projects in all of the subject areas. (There is a copy of this unit in Appendix B on p. 133.) To learn science, students conducted experiments with gum using the scientific method. In math, we conducted estimation games, guessing how many gumballs were in a jar using mathematical theory. In social studies, we looked at the history of gum and how it has changed over the year, even researching gum laws. The English side of the project involved looking at and writing poetry that dealt with how people felt about gum. These were fun activities that I did not grade, so the students felt no pressure. And because they got to chew lots of gum, they looked at the project as something fun, rather than feeling anxiety about something new. (Of course, some administrators and parents may be wary of a project involving gum chewing, so you might modify the project or come up with one involving less sugary fare.) Once we had spent a couple of weeks on this fun project, I introduced the other projects using the same structure.

When it comes to managing day-to-day stress, you have to learn to read the language, both verbal and nonverbal, of your students. Obviously, some students will need more maintenance than others. You might have an insecure student who needs hundreds of questions answered. You want to answer as many of these questions as it takes to inspire the student's confidence while still leaving enough questions unanswered for the student to develop independence. You might have another student who doesn't say a word, but is struggling nonetheless. You must be vigilant about detecting confusion even in the absence of questions, for without guidance, some students will continue to flounder and will grow quite frustrated and defeated. PBL is often useful for these students, who fly under the radar more easily in a traditional classroom than in a PBL classroom, with its one-on-one conferencing. You will do far more observing in the PBL classroom than you may be used to, looking for signs that students are encountering roadblocks. Signs that a student is struggling include lots of sighing, a lack of productivity, and being off task or overwhelmed. Be careful not to discipline students too quickly, because incidents of disruptive behavior might be subtle cries for help. Instead, inquire as to whether the behavior is a result of insecurities about working on projects.

GIVING STUDENTS SPACE

Probably one of the most difficult things for teachers to do when adjusting from being traditional classroom teachers to being PBL teachers is the need to give students space. We are used to monitoring everything that our students are doing and checking to make sure that students are doing what they ought to be doing. Being that the brunt of the responsibility is on the students in a PBL classroom, you have to allow them the space to stretch out and use this responsibility to their advantage. As Stix and Hrbek (2006), in their fine book *Teachers as Classroom Coaches: How to Motivate Students Across the Content Areas*, pointed out:

> Good teacher-coaches are always patient, supportive, attentive, genuinely interested, and aware of what is important in a lesson. For this to be the case, coaches must remain somewhat detached from the activities at hand; rather than take ownership of the process, they should allow students to make their own way. (p. 28)

What this boils down to is less monitoring in the classroom. Students shouldn't feel as though you are breathing down their necks or setting deadlines every single class. Students need to have the physical and mental space required to research, to struggle, and even to fail. That is one of the best methods of learning, struggling with something and then overcoming it. As the teacher-coach, you want to be close enough that if you see them drowning, you can throw them a line. But you also need to be far enough away to let them panic a little and figure out how to tread water. Students will take much more ownership over a project if they are the ones who figure out how to succeed.

Sometimes, as the coach, you have to be more observant of students' body language than their actual language. If a student is sitting slumped over, he may be experiencing frustration and need a helping hand. If a student is focused and attentive to what she is working on, it is probably best just to leave her alone, lest you risk interrupting her concentration.

KEEPING STUDENTS' EYES ON THE PRIZE

One of the most important tasks involved with project-based learning as a coach is to keep students focused on the learning outcomes at hand. Particularly when students are working on products that allow them to be very creative, they can sometimes get so caught up in the product that they lose sight of what they are supposed to be learning. A wise teacher once told me, "Even if the student can produce a drawing of the Mona Lisa comparable to the one produced by Da Vinci, if it doesn't teach what was intended, then it didn't accomplish anything." Be sure that the students are always connecting the product to the learning outcome of the project. This is why we link the projects to learning outcomes and state standards in the first place. As the teacher-coach, you have the responsibility of checking over the products from time to time to be sure that students are on the correct path.

In a PBL environment, the challenge is to figure out ways to keep students focused on the task at hand without interrupting the entire class. You might post the learning outcome(s) on the board so students have a constant reminder of their objective, you might refer students to their rubrics as much as possible so that they understand what they should be focusing on, or you might mention the learning outcome explicitly in the students' contracts. Partner students with project buddies who can check over each other's products and remind each other to look for the learning outcome. I always have students conduct a second evaluation with a parent, an older sibling, or another teacher so that someone else is seeing the student's product before it is finalized and submitted. When you conference with students, always ask them what it is they are supposed to be learning to see that they really get it. Then ask them to explain how their research or product is accomplishing this learning goal. This will focus students and reinforce the learning outcome.

CONFERENCING

A nice thing about PBL is that you will be able to meet with each student individually through conferencing. This allows for check-in points throughout the process. In a traditional classroom, sometimes the teacher does not know whether students are getting the subject matter, often until the end-of-unit test. It may be too late at this point to remedy any gaps in knowledge, because students must quickly move on to another topic. Wouldn't it be more effective and powerful if students received the instruction for correction *during* the creation of the project so they could adjust and learn from it? According to Goldsmith (1997), if a business manager relies completely on performance reviews given at the end of a review period to improve the quality of employees' work, an improvement can be made of about 46%–48%. But if that same manager follows up on the report, conferencing with employees throughout the period and responding to any concerns they may have, that improvement rate increases to as much as 95%, quite substantial growth. That is the power of conferencing. By speaking individually with students and responding to them on a case-by-case basis, you will help them to adjust and improve, making for better learning.

Another thing you will find when conferencing with students is that you will get to know them better. Because the teacher's role in a traditional classroom is to teach and oversee the group, the only way we learn about individual performance is via assessment or via behavior that sets a student apart from the pack—often negative behavior. As a result, those quiet students who stay out of trouble or do not participate in classroom discussion can disappear into the background. Individual conferencing lets you be personable with all students and modifies your mentality: Rather than addressing a group, you tailor your questions for a specific student. As O'Neil and Hopkins (2002) pointed out, coaching "allows the student-teacher relationship to develop on a deeper level . . . and provides an opportunity for the teacher to step out of the expert mode and engage with the students in a process of co-inquiry" (p. 407).

When offering advice to a student, it is important not to offer too much—otherwise, you risk overwhelming the student. When I began coaching tennis, I might advise one of my players, "You need to get your service toss up, attack your opponent's backhand, and move your feet better." Although all three of these pieces of advice were warranted and could improve the player's game if addressed, my player would go out on the court and forget most of what I had said, because I had given too much advice, causing it to become jumbled and ignored. I learned after a few years of experience to give the player just one piece of advice to focus on. After the player had worked on footwork, then it was time to work on the service toss.

The same goes for the classroom. For instance, consider a student who has organization problems, often forgets to cite her sources, and makes lots of spelling errors. If you advised her to fix all three problems at once, she might become overwhelmed and exert a halfhearted effort in all three areas, accomplishing little. Instead, the two of you could discuss the most pressing issue and focus on that first. Let's say that together, you decided that organization was the most important issue. You could help her organize herself simply by using headings to separate information, or by using a single notebook to keep track of her notes. Once she had become accustomed to doing these things, you could move on to another issue, such as citing sources.

COACHING STUDENTS IN GROUP WORK

If you are having students work in groups in PBL, there will need to be deliberate coaching so that the groups are efficient and produce quality work. Many times, we as teachers just throw students together and expect them to be able to work together. Sometimes this happens, but there are times when it does not. As the teacher-coach, you must be deliberate about how you teach students to work in groups and support them.

At the beginning of the year, I have each student complete an activity or activities to indicate what sort of learner that student is. This may take the shape of completing learning inventories online or reading over a list of student profiles and selecting which description best fits. Two such activities, Compass Points and Profile of a Student, can be found in Appendix B on pages 128 and 130. In these activities, students identify themselves as learners with particular strengths, weaknesses, and preferences. They also recognize that there are advantages and disadvantages to their learning styles, and they figure out how they work best. Once the students understand how they learn and work best, they can share this with their group members and brainstorm ideas for how to best work with them. Developing understanding and tolerance among group members goes a long way towards figuring out how to make the group work.

A common mistake that people make when it comes to group work is to give all of the group members equal tasks and equal amounts of work to do. Although this seems fair, it often is not, because it puts certain students at a disadvantage. All group members are not necessarily equal when it comes to skills. Educators of the gifted should be especially familiar with this problem: When educated is targeted towards average students, the weaker students continue to struggle, and the gifted students are perpetually bored. The solution, of course, is to differentiate to reach the various levels. The same goes for students working in groups. Group members have different strengths and weaknesses. If you have a student who learns visually and is good at technology, have that student design the PowerPoint. If you have someone who is good at detail, put that person in charge of organizing the research. If you have a student who is quiet and is terrified of speaking in front of people, don't have that student be part of the oral presentation. The first thing a group needs is to understand one another, and subsequently to divide up tasks based on strengths and learning styles. This does not mean that if someone is lazy, that person should not be assigned work. Rather, it means that finding strengths and dispensing tasks according to these strengths will result in the best overall experience and product for the group.

Once students understand their own strengths, allow them to practice working in groups in a situation where there isn't too much on the line. This can mean working on an introductory project, it can mean working on an activity designed to have students meet a specific goal, or it can mean a team-building activity. I often use a simulation in which students must come to a consensus in a group in order to make a decision. Each person gets different information and must communicate this information to the other members before the group decides together what route to take. This activity allows students to put into practice what they have learned about working with others and using communication. Each group then appoints someone to be the spokesperson, another person to record the group's answers, and so on. If you conduct a similar activity, be sure to debrief often with groups to help them analyze what works and what does not.

Revisit how to work successfully in groups from time to time throughout the year. Constant reminders about how to work successfully in groups, such as signs around the room or forming group norms, might be helpful. I print out a list of tips (included in Appendix A on p. 97) for working in groups that students keep in their folders and refer to throughout the year. Just like an atmosphere for independent learning must be deliberate, so must be an atmosphere of collaboration.

Once students begin to work together on actual projects, you can have sit-down conferences with groups to make sure that they are on task. Use contracts with groups in which they break the project down into separate parts, and list which roles everyone will be playing, to help maintain focus.

You must also give groups space to figure things out for themselves. A group might have a group member who is not contributing enough, causing the other students to become frustrated. Rather than going over to the group and making this student get to work, you should allow the group to figure out a way to encourage this student to offer more. You should only intervene when it is clear that the group has reached an impasse and cannot move forward until the issue has been resolved.

IN A NUTSHELL

The role of the teacher in a PBL classroom is very different than it is in a traditional classroom. The teacher, rather than being an enforcer, is a coach. Rather than jumping into the middle of the action, the coach must guide from the sidelines. This guidance comes in the form of:

- managing stress,
- giving students space,
- keeping students focused, and
- conferencing.

PBL allows for a lot of one-on-one time with students. Sometimes, you must coach an entire group, applying the same techniques as you would with individual students. By running the class in this manner, you allow students to take responsibility themselves, and you empower them as learners. These are very important skills—not only in the PBL classroom, but also in life.

CONCLUSION

Empowering Students

■ ■ ■ ■ ■ ■ ■ ■ ■ ■ ■ ■ ■

The introduction of this book promised that project-based learning would provide at least four benefits for your gifted classroom:

- increased creativity,
- differentiation for varying ability levels,
- motivation for underachieving students, and
- passion for learning.

Let's reflect to see how we did.

Does PBL allow for more creativity? Students are given choices regarding which products best demonstrate what they have learned, offering them a lot of opportunities to be creative. A student with a gift for music might compose a song, a technology guru might create a website, and a student with a knack for drama might write a play. The ceiling that pencil-and-paper tests place on creativity is lifted in the PBL classroom, allowing students to explore territory outside of the box more frequently and in more depth.

Does PBL allow for differentiation, enabling students of varying ability levels to learn at their own pace? There is a wide range of ability levels even within the gifted community. A teacher who assumes that all gifted students should be taught at the same level is likely unfamiliar with just how different students can be from one another, not only regarding degree of giftedness, but also regarding learning style, personality, and interests. Just as much differentiation, if not more, needs to take place in the gifted classroom as occurs in the typical classroom. PBL provides differentiation naturally, because it allows students to explore topics in as much depth as they like, given that students are creating their own products and conducting their own research. Given the proper project structure and coaching, students can set high goals for themselves and even surpass those goals. The products will have them working above the knowledge level, the comprehension level, and even the application level of Bloom's taxonomy, taking them to the higher levels of analysis, synthesis, and evaluation.

Does PBL motivate underachieving gifted students? One of the leading causes of underachievement among gifted students is boredom. These students become bored with the classroom because they are moving at such a slow pace compared to what they are capable of, and they cease to learn in school. What if these same students could learn at whatever pace they set for themselves? Another cause of underachievement in gifted students is a lack of motivation, many times due to a lack of interest in the topic that causes them to stop paying attention in class. Because projects allow students to explore various facets of topics, once a student has achieved the basic concept of a project, then the student could pursue another aspect of the topic, going into more depth. Giving students a choice in what they study and pursue, an option not often afforded them in a traditional learning environment, motivates students and gives them control over their education.

Does PBL create a passion for learning? In many ways, the traditional classroom fails to create learners. Rather, it creates memorizers, test takers, worksheet filler-inners, and other masters of inside-the-box methods of thinking, students who have learned to play the game of school. Because PBL empowers students to take responsibility for their own learning, students develop ownership over their learning. It is *their* learning. And because the learning belongs to the students, the students will develop a greater passion for it. The greatest thing about PBL is that it teaches students *how* to learn, not *what* to learn. This is knowledge that students can carry outside of the classroom and apply to anything in their lives. Anything that a student wants to know more about can be explored using the skills learned in a PBL classroom. If a student remains in an environment where a teacher provides everything, what will that student do when nobody is around to supply information? How will the student find the necessary information? PBL, rather than supplying students with fish, teaches them to fish for themselves.

My final piece of advice is this: Go forth and teach your students to fish. Your students will become better students, and you may find yourself becoming a better teacher.

References

■ ■ ■ ■ ■ ■ ■ ■ ■ ■ ■ ■

Anderson, L., & Krathwohl, D. A. (Eds.). (2001). *Taxonomy for learning, teaching, and assessing: A revision of Bloom's taxonomy of educational objectives.* New York, NY: Longman.

Bastiaens, T., & Martens, R. (2000). Conditions for web-based learning with real events. In B. Abbey (Ed.), *Instructional and cognitive impacts of web-based education* (pp. 1–32). Hershley/London: Idea Group Publishing.

Bloom, B. S., Engelhart, M. D., Furst, E. J., Hill, W. H., & Krathwohl, D. R. (1956). *Taxonomy of educational objectives: The classification of educational goals; Handbook I: Cognitive domain.* New York, NY: Longman, Green & Co.

Brewer, C. B. (2008). *Soundtracks for learning: Using music in the classroom.* Bellingham, WA: LifeSounds Educational Services.

Buck Institute for Education. (2011). *Does PBL work?* Retrieved from http://www.bie.org/research/does_pbl_work

California State Board of Education. (2007). *English-language arts content standards for California public schools: Kindergarten through grade twelve.* Sacramento, CA: California Department of Education.

Centre for Teaching Excellence. (n.d.). *University of Waterloo CTE teaching tips.* Retrieved from http://cte.uwaterloo.ca/teaching_resources/tips/self-directed_learning_learning_contracts.html

Common Core State Standards Initiative. (2010). *Mathematics, grade 1, measurement & data.* Retrieved from http://www.corestandards.org/the-standards/mathematics/grade-1/measurement-and-data

Connecticut Math Standards. (2010). *Patterns and functions.* Retrieved from http://www.mathscore.com/math/standards/Connecticut/1st%20Grade

Connecticut State Department of Education. (2009). *Connecticut social studies curriculum framework grades PK–12.* Retrieved from http://www.sde.ct.gov/sde/lib/sde/pdf/curriculum/socialstudies/ssfrmwk_10-6-09.pdf

Council for Exceptional Children. (2010). *Time management for gifted kids*. Retrieved from http://school.familyeducation.com/organization/gifted-education/38344.html

Dunn, R., Dunn, K., & Price, G. E. (1984). *Learning style inventory*. Lawrence, KS: Price Systems.

Explore Knowledge Academy. (2006). *About EKA*. Retrieved from http://www.ekacademy.org/about

Goldsmith, M. (1997). Ask, learn, follow-up, and grow. In F. Hesselbein, M. Goldsmith, & R. Beckhard (Eds.), *The Drucker Foundation: Leader of the future* (pp. 227–237). San Francisco, CA: Jossey-Bass.

Grant, M. M., & Branch, R. M. (2005). Project-based learning in middle school: Tracing abilities through the artifacts of learning. *Journal of Research on Technology in Education, 38*, 65–98.

Horton, R. M., Hedetniemi, T., Wiegert, E., & Wagner, J. R. (2006). Integrating curriculum through themes. *Mathematics Teaching in the Middle School, 11*, 408–414.

Johnsen-Harris, M. A. (1983). Surviving the budget crunch from an independent school perspective. *Roeper Review, 6*, 79–81.

Johnston, D. E. (2004). Measurement, scale, and theater arts. *Mathematics Teaching in the Middle School, 9*, 412–417.

Jones, B. F., Rasmussen, C. M., & Moffit, M. C. (1997). *Real-life problem solving: A collaborative approach to interdisciplinary learning*. Washington, DC: American Psychological Association.

Jones, G., & Kalinowski, K. (2007). Touring Mars online, real-time, in 3-D, for math and science educators and students. *Journal of Computers in Mathematics and Science Teaching, 26*, 123–136.

Karnes, F. A., & Stephens, K. R. (2009). *The Ultimate Guide for Student Product Development and Evaluation*. Waco, TX: Prufrock Press.

Kingsley, R. F. (1986). "Digging" for understanding and significance: A high school enrichment model. *Roeper Review, 9*, 37–38.

Ljung, E. J., & Blackwell, M. (1996). Project OMEGA: A winning approach for at-risk teens. *Illinois School Research and Development Journal, 33*(1), 15–17.

Louisiana Department of Education. (2010). *Louisiana's content standards, benchmarks, and grade level expectations for science*. Retrieved from http://www.doa.louisiana.gov/osr/lac/28v123/28v123.pdf

Missouri Department of Elementary and Secondary Education. (2008). *Mathematics grade- and course-level expectations*. Retrieved from http://dese.mo.gov/divimprove/curriculum/GLE/documents/ma_gle_2.0_k8_0408.pdf

Matthews, D. J., & Foster, J. F. (2005). *Being smart about gifted children: A guidebook for parents and educators*. Scottsdale, AZ: Great Potential Press.

McMiller, T., Lee, T., Saroop, R., Green, T., & Johnson, C. M. (2006). Middle/high school students in the research laboratory: A summer internship program emphasizing the interdisciplinary nature of biology. *Biochemistry and Molecular Biology Education, 34*, 88–93.

O'Neil, D. A., & Hopkins, M. M. (2002). The teacher as coach approach: Pedagogical choices for management educators. *Journal of Management Education, 26*, 402–414.

Ohio Department of Education. (2002). *Academic content standards*. Retrieved from http://www.ode.state.oh.us/GD/Templates/Pages/ODE/ODEDetail.aspx?Page=3&TopicRelationID=1705&Content=100394

Peterson, M. (1997). Skills to enhance problem-based learning. *Medical Education Online, 2*(3). Retrieved from http://med-ed-online.net/index.php/meo/article/view/4289

Project School. (2011). *Assessment*. Retrieved from http://indianapolisprojectschool.org/index.php?option=com_content&view=article&id=20&Itemid=53

Public Schools of North Carolina. (2006). *North Carolina standard course of study: Social studies*. Retrieved from http://www.ncpublicschools.org/docs/curriculum/socialstudies/scos/socialstudies.pdf

Renzulli, J. S., Smith, L. H., & Reis, S. M. (1982). Curriculum compacting: An essential strategy for working with gifted students. *The Elementary School Journal, 82,* 185–194.

Rogers, K. B. (2002). *Re-forming gifted education: How parents and teachers can match the program to their child*. Scottsdale, AZ: Great Potential Press.

Siegle, D., & McCoach, D. B. (2005). Making a difference: Motivating gifted students who are not achieving. *Teaching Exceptional Children, 38*(1), 22–27.

Stewart, E. D. (1981). Learning styles among gifted/talented students: Instructional technique preferences. *Exceptional Children, 48,* 134–138.

Stix, A., & Hrbek, F. (2006). *Teachers and classroom coaches: How to motivate students across the content areas*. Alexandria, VA: Association for Supervision and Curriculum Development.

Stoof, A., Martens, R. L., Merriënboer, J. J. G., & Bastiaens, T. J. (2002). The boundary approach of competence: A constructivist aid for understanding and using the concept of competence. *Human Resource Development Review, 1,* 345–365.

Thomas, J. W. (2000). *A review of research on project-based learning*. San Rafael, CA: The Autodesk Foundation.

Thompson-Grove, G. (n.d.). *Profile of a student activity: Student Profiles*. Retrieved from http://www.nsrfharmony.org/protocol/doc/student_profiles.pdf

Toolin, R. E. (2004). Striking a balance between innovation and standards: A study of teachers implementing project-based approaches to teaching science. *Journal of Science Education and Technology, 13,* 179–187.

Virginia Department of Education. (2010). *Virginia state standards of learning*. Retrieved from http://www.doe.virginia.gov/testing/sol/standards_docs/english/2010/stds_english9.pdf

Whitener, E. M. (1989). A meta-analytic review of the effect of learning on the interaction between prior achievement and instructional support. *Review of Educational Research, 59,* 65–86.

Whitney, C. S., & Hirsch, G. (2007). *A love for learning: Motivation and the gifted child*. Scottsdale, AZ: Great Potential Press.

Wiggins, G., & McTighe, J. (2001). *Understanding by design*. Upper Saddle River, NJ: Prentice Hall.

Zimmerman, B. J. (1989). A social cognitive view of self-regulated academic learning. *Journal of Educational Psychology, 81,* 329–339.

APPENDIX

Reproducibles

■ ■ ■ ■ ■ ■ ■ ■ ■ ■ ■ ■ ■

These reproducibles may be used with a wide variety of grade levels. You may wish to alter or adapt them to fit to your specific classroom or purposes.

CALENDAR #1

Student Name: _____

Name of Project: _____

Due Date of Project: _____

Day _____	Day _____	Day _____	Day _____	Day _____
Day _____	Day _____	Day _____	Day _____	Day _____
Day _____	Day _____	Day _____	Day _____	Day _____
Day _____	Day _____	Day _____	Day _____	Day _____

CALENDAR #2

SUN	MON	TUE	WED	THU	FRI	SAT

PROJECT CONTRACT

Student Name:_____

Project Name: _____

Estimated Time of Project (Attach Calendar): _____

Standard(s) Covered: _____

Skills Learned:

-   _____
-   _____
-   _____
-   _____

Overall Goal of Project:_____

_____

_____

Product of Project: _____

_____

Student Signature:_____

Teacher's Signature: _____

Parent(s) Signature:_____

STUDENT CONTRACT

Student Name:_____

Learning Experience: _____

What are you going to learn? (Objectives)	How are you going to learn it? (Resources and Strategies)	By when will you learn it? (Completion Date)	How are you going to show that you learned it? (Evidence)	How are you going to prove that you learned it? (Verification)	Advising faculty member feedback (Evaluation)
Itemize what you want to be able to do or know at the end of this project.	What do you have to do in order meet each of the objectives defined?	By when do you plan to complete each task?	What is the specific task that you will complete to demonstrate learning?	Who will receive the product of your learning, and how will that person evaluate it?	How well was the task completed? Provide an assessment decision.

I have reviewed and find acceptable the above learning contract.

Student Signature:_____ Date:_____

Teacher Signature: _____ Date:_____

From "Self-Directed Learning: Learning Contracts," by the Centre for Teaching Excellence at the University of Waterloo, n.d. Retrieved from http://cte.uwaterloo.ca/teaching_resources/tips/self-directed_learning_learning_contracts.html. Adapted with permission.

BLOOM'S TAXONOMY KEY WORDS

Knowledge	*choose, define, find, how, identify, label, list, locate, name, omit, recall, recognize, select, show, spell, tell, what, when, where, which, who, why*
Comprehension	*add, compare, describe, distinguish, explain, express, extend, illustrate, outline, paraphrase, relate, rephrase, summarize, translate, understand*
Application	*answer, apply, build, choose, conduct, construct, demonstrate, design, develop, experiment with, illustrate, interpret, interview, make use of, model, organize, plan, present, produce, respond, solve*
Analysis	*analyze, assume, categorize, classify, compare and contrast, conclude, deduce, discover, dissect, distinguish, edit, examine, explain, function, infer, inspect, motive, reason, test for, validate*
Synthesis	*build, change, combine, compile, compose, construct, create, design, develop, discuss, estimate, formulate, hypothesize, imagine, integrate, invent, make up, modify, originate, organize, plan, predict, propose, rearrange, revise, suppose, theorize*
Evaluation	*appraise, assess, award, conclude, criticize, debate, defend, determine, disprove, evaluate, give opinion, interpret, judge, justify, influence, prioritize, prove, recommend, support, verify*

INTERNET SEARCH SCAVENGER HUNT

1. You need to find information about who has the most home runs ever in baseball. Using Google (http://www.google.com), enter the search term "baseball." How many matches do you get? _____ What key terms could you use to narrow your search?

    _____

    _____

    Run the search again with these key terms. How many matches do you have now? _____ Who holds the home run record, and how many does he have?

    _____

2. You need to find an image. Go to Bing (http://www.bing.com). Put in the search term "ancient maps of Mesopotamia." Find an image that shows the two rivers that formed the borders of the Mesopotamian civilization. What are they?

    _____

3. You need to find the deepest river in the world. Go to Yahoo! (http://yahoo.com) and put in the search term "deepest river in the world." Go to the Yahoo! Answers website (http://www.answers.yahoo.com). What answer does it give? _____ Now go to the Wiki Answers website (http://www.wiki.answers.com). What answer does it give? _____ Research further to determine what the correct answer is. What is the correct answer, and how did you find it?_____

    _____

    _____

4. Go to the search engine Ask (http://www.ask.com). Put in the search question, "What is the lost planet?" How many pages do you have to go through until you find a site that deals with the rumored lost planet of the solar system? _____ What is the name of that planet? _____

5. Go to the online encyclopedia Wikipedia (http://www.wikipedia.org). Put in a search for the term "physical change." What is an example provided of a physical change? _____ Conduct your own search and find five better examples for what a physical change is. Write the name of your source after each number.

    1. _____

    2. _____

    3. _____

    4. _____

    5. _____

6. Go to the following website:
   http://militaryhistory.about.com/od/americanrevolution/a/amrevcauses.htm
   Search the article and summarize in your own words what it says about the Intolerable Acts.

   _____

   _____

   _____

   _____

   _____

   _____

7. Go to the following website:
   http://en.wikipedia.org/wiki/Radiocarbon_dating
   Put the information on carbon dating into your own words.

   _____

   _____

   _____

   _____

   _____

   _____

   Using a different search engine, find a website that offers a simpler explanation of carbon dating and summarize it in your own words. Mention the search engine(s) you used.

   _____

   _____

   _____

   _____

   _____

   _____

TIPS FOR WORKING IN GROUPS

Celebrate differences. If everyone was the same, everyone would have the same ideas, and there would be no creativity or variety.

Give everyone a chance. There will be some dominant personalities in the group. Let those quiet people contribute, as well. Try passing a pen around—whoever holds it gets to speak uninterrupted.

Ideas belong to the group, not the individual. When you share an idea, it becomes the property of the group and can be changed and altered to fit the group's needs.

Make sure everyone feels like a part of the group. Even if you do not take someone's suggestions, honor that person's contribution. When people feel valued, they do better work, and everybody is worthy of respect.

BLANK RUBRIC

Student: _____

Project: _____

	Excellent	Good	Needs Improvement

EXAMPLE OF JOURNAL RUBRIC

Student: _____

	Journal	Content	Responsibility
Excellent	▪ Student follows the format of the journal assignments (e.g., poem, list, essay, role-play). ▪ Student is creative with the journal entries. ▪ Student's journal captures what has been learned using specific examples.	▪ Student includes many details designed to back up points. ▪ Entries are well thought out, with insights and examples from the student's own perspective. ▪ Student not only completes the assignment, but also goes above and beyond the expectations.	▪ All entries in the journal are completed. ▪ Journal is turned in on time. ▪ Student uses time given in class well, staying focused.
Good	▪ Student follows the format of most of the journal assignments, but not all of them. ▪ Student completes the assignment but does not use much creativity, instead just following the directions. ▪ Student's journal captures what has been learned but does not use many specific examples to back up points.	▪ Student has some details to back up points, but could use more. ▪ Student provides some insights and examples from own perspective, but misses opportunities to add others. ▪ Student completes the assignment, but gives no extra effort toward the entry.	▪ Student has all journal entries, but some are incomplete. ▪ Journal is turned in one day late. ▪ Student uses time in class well, but loses focus occasionally.
Needs Improvement	▪ Student does not follow the format of the journal assignments. ▪ Student is not creative in any way, making bland entries. ▪ Student's journal does not capture what has been learned and offers few to no examples.	▪ Student does not use details to back up points. ▪ Students does not include insights or examples from own perspective. ▪ Student makes a half-hearted effort to complete the journal, providing the bare minimum or less.	▪ Student is missing one or more of the journal entries. ▪ Student turns in the journal more than one day late. ▪ Student makes poor use of class time, losing focus or not writing during the time provided.

EXAMPLE OF RESEARCH PAPER RUBRIC

Student: _____   Topic: _____

Overall	Content	Grammar/Spelling	Research
Excellent	▪ Student explains points clearly, providing much detail. ▪ Student uses many examples to illustrate the points made in the paper. ▪ Student appears to be an expert on the topic(s) researched, not just putting down the basics, but also showing an understanding of them.	▪ Paper has few to no spelling/grammatical errors. ▪ Paper uses a sentence structure that makes the paragraphs flow, and paper is easy to read. ▪ Paper follows a clear outline, allowing the reader to know what is being discussed at any given time.	▪ A complete bibliography is included. ▪ Research comes from a variety of sources (at least five), pulling from all of them for paper's content. ▪ Research is consistently put into student's own words, paraphrasing the information.
Good	▪ Student explains the assigned topic but does not provide enough detail to make it clear. ▪ Student uses a few examples to illustrate the points made in the paper, but needs more to make points clearer. ▪ Student appears to have a good grasp on the topic researched, putting down the basics and seeming to understand them.	▪ Paper has occasional spelling/grammatical errors, including more than a handful of mistakes. ▪ Paper generally uses a sentence structure that makes the paragraphs flow and the paper easy to read, but has the occasional awkward sentence that causes confusion. ▪ Paper follows an outline, but doesn't always allow the reader to know what is being discussed at any given time.	▪ Bibliography is included but is not complete. ▪ Research comes from a variety of sources (at least five), but relies heavily on one of them for most the content. ▪ Research is put into student's own words, paraphrasing the information, but occasionally using others' terms and phrases.
Needs Improvement	▪ Student does not always explain the assigned topic, straying from the topic or lacking details, making points unclear. ▪ Student uses very few examples to illustrate the points made in the paper, making it confusing or unclear. ▪ Student does not seem to understand the topic researched, having just the basics and not seeming to understand them.	▪ Paper has many spelling/grammatical errors, making it difficult to read the paper at times. ▪ Paper has a sloppy sentence structure that makes the paragraphs difficult to follow and the content unclear. ▪ Paper does not follow a clear outline, causing the reader confusion about what is being discussed at any given time.	▪ Bibliography is very incomplete or is not included. ▪ Research comes from a limited number of sources (fewer than five) and relies heavily on one of them for most the content. ▪ Research is many times not put into student's own words, using terms and phrases awkwardly.

Student: _____ Topic: _____

EXAMPLE OF PRESENTATION RUBRIC

Overall	Content	Presentation	Visual Aid
Excellent	■ Includes many details to clarify points. ■ Has many examples designed to back up content and points. ■ Research is from reliable sources.	■ Speaker presents clearly and does not read to audience. ■ Speaker makes consistent eye contact with audience. ■ Speaker is confident in presentation and is able to answer all questions.	■ Uses meaningful visuals that expand on and complement the content. ■ Visual aids can be seen clearly by all audience members. ■ There are several visual aids from many sources.
Good	■ Includes details to clarify points in most cases, but occasionally there is a lapse in clarity due to a lack of details. ■ Has some examples to back up points, but could use more. ■ Most of research is from reliable sources, but some research is questionable or not correct.	■ Speaker presents clearly most of the time but reads the presentation occasionally. ■ Speaker makes eye contact with audience but occasionally looks down. ■ Speaker is confident for most of the presentation and can answer all questions but a few.	■ Uses visuals, but not all of them are meaningful, with some serving more for decoration than for elaboration. ■ Most visual aids can be seen by all audience members, but a few are difficult to make out. ■ Presentation includes good number of visual aids, but some parts could have used visual aids or different visual aids.
Needs Improvement	■ Does not include much detail, making the points the student is trying to make confusing. ■ Uses few to no examples to back up points. ■ Much of student's research comes from questionable sources or is incorrect.	■ Speaker reads the entire presentation or cannot be heard. ■ Speaker stares at note cards, rarely making eye contact with the audience. ■ Speaker is not confident and has difficulty answering most questions.	■ Presentation lacks visuals or includes visuals that do not complement the content. ■ Many of the visuals are difficult to see. ■ There are very few or no visuals.

APPENDIX

Lessons

■ ■ ■ ■ ■ ■ ■ ■ ■ ■ ■ ■

The following materials may be helpful as you introduce project-based learning to your classroom. The included examples of projects may be used as they are, or they may inspire you to create your own. Many of the included materials are reproducible.

MINI-PROJECT: PAPER VERSUS PLASTIC

For this science project, you will work with your group members to conduct research, create a product, and present your findings to the class.

QUESTIONS:

- What are the advantages or disadvantages of using paper grocery bags?
- What are the advantages or disadvantages of using plastic grocery bags?
- Which of the two do you think is best to use and why?
- Is there a third alternative that would be better than paper or plastic?

MATERIALS:

- Assignment sheet
- Articles concerning the use of paper and plastic

POSSIBLE PRODUCTS:

- Lesson
- Game
- Presentation (PowerPoint)
- Simulation
- Demonstration
- A product of your group's choosing

To complete this project, you should figure out how to divide up tasks among your group members and stick to the schedule:

- _____ minutes for inquiry, exploration, and research

- _____ minutes to create a product

- _____ minutes for each group to present

You will have to be focused as you research and create your product, and you will need to be concise when you present. Be respectful of other groups as they are making their presentations. In class discussions, be sure to offer criticism in a constructive way and be receptive to others' suggestions.

PROJECT STRUCTURE: SINGLE SUBJECT

Here is the structure I used in my fifth- and sixth-grade science classes. I break the structure down into four phases for students so that it is not so overwhelming. This same structure would work well for students in high school, but if you are teaching younger students, you may wish to break down the structure even further to provide additional guidance.

PHASE I: SETUP

This is where students will decide what projects they will be working on and how much time they will give themselves to complete their projects. There are two aspects of the setup phase: rubrics and calendars.

Students can choose from the following products:
1. Demonstration
2. Electronic portfolio
3. Essay
4. Exhibition
5. Journal
6. Research paper
7. Presentation
8. Portfolio
9. Performance
10. Test

Each student has to create and provide a rubric that will be used to evaluate the selected product. The calendar will plot out the day-by-day course of the project and will include checkpoints and deadlines. Both the rubric and the calendar must be approved before the student can begin.

PHASE II: RESEARCH

This is the part of the project where students go into more depth and address the learning standard(s), seeking a true understanding of the topic. Students will use books and the Internet to compile information needed to understand the various objectives.

Every day there will be conferencing sessions during which notes will be checked and questions can be answered.

PHASE III: PRODUCT

Students will spend this time creating the products they have chosen to show what they have learned.

Products students may choose include the following:
1. Demonstration
2. Electronic portfolio
3. Essay
4. Exhibition
5. Journal
6. Research paper
7. Presentation
8. Portfolio
9. Performance
10. Test

PHASE IV: ASSESSMENT

Here, students will demonstrate what they have learned with their products. They must also include an evaluation. The student should either complete a self-evaluation or select an option from the following list of parties who might evaluate the student:
1. Another teacher
2. A student peer
3. A panel
4. A parent or relative
5. A mentor
6. An expert

PROJECT STRUCTURE: MULTIPLE SUBJECTS

This is the project structure that I developed for the Ivy Program, a one-day-a-week gifted pullout program for third and fourth graders. Because I only got to see students once a week, I was very purposeful about the calendar and making sure students that were working on their projects for at least 15 minutes every day. I knew from experience that without this link to their projects, students would forget about them from week to week and would lose their enthusiasm. For examples of projects I have used, see pages 112–122.

STEP 1

- Each student should select a project that he or she finds interesting.
    - o At any given time, there are 20 projects to choose from.
    - o Projects vary across different content areas, most of them containing elements from multiple disciplines.
    - o Different students can be working on the same project, either together or independently.
    - o Projects will be rotated every couple of weeks or so to ensure there are always fresh ones available for students.

STEP 2

- Have students locate the standards their projects will cover.
    - o Rather than dictating the standards to the students, have them look through the standards and identify which ones they will be working to meet as they complete their projects.
    - o It will be obvious to students how some standards are connected to projects, while the links between projects and other standards might be subtler.
    - o Students will record the standards they intend to meet on a project sheet.

STEP 3

- Each student should determine the goals, skills, and products of the project.
    - o Each student will fill out a project contract and gain teacher and parent/guardian approval.
    - o The contract should specify the student's goals and what the final product will look like.

PROJECT CONTRACT

Student Name:_____

Project Name: _____

Estimated Time of Project (Attach Calendar): _____

Standard(s) Covered: _____

Skills Learned:

- _____
- _____
- _____
- _____

Overall Goal of Project:_____

_____

_____

Product of Project:_____

_____

How Project Will Be Evaluated (Attach Rubric): _____

_____

Student Signature:_____

Teacher Signature: _____

Signature of Parent or Guardian: _____

STEP 4

- Students should plot out on calendars how they will execute their projects.
  - o This will help organize the students on a day-to-day basis so they know what they must accomplish and by when.
  - o This is particularly helpful for visual learners.

STEP 5

- Students should create their own rubrics describing how their projects and products will be evaluated.
  - o Because students create these rubrics themselves, the expectations will be absolutely clear to them.
  - o A workshop at the beginning of the year or project will show students how to create their own rubrics.
  - o Students will review their rubrics with the teacher to ensure that they have made useful, reasonable rubrics.

STEP 6

- Students will complete their daily tasks and will fill out logs.
  - o This will keep students focused on their goals and will help their organization.
  - o This will help students who tend to get distracted or lose track of their goals.

Student:_____   Date: _____

PROJECT LOG

DAY 1

Goal that I will accomplish by the end of the day:

_____

_____

How I will achieve this goal:

_____

_____

Verification that I achieved this goal:

_____
Signature of teacher or advisor

DAY 2

Goal that I will accomplish by the end of the day:

_____

_____

How I will achieve this goal:

_____

_____

Verification that I achieved this goal:

_____
Signature of teacher or advisor

DAY 3

Goal that I will accomplish by the end of the day:

_____

_____

How I will achieve this goal:

_____

_____

Verification that I achieved this goal:

_____
Signature of teacher or advisor

STEP 7

- At the end of the project, students present the products they decided on at the beginning of the project.
  - o Students can present these products to:
    - the teacher,
    - parents,
    - fellow classmates,
    - fellow students,
    - community members, and
    - experts in the field.

EXAMPLES OF PROJECTS

The 10 projects that follow are examples of projects I developed for students over the years. Because this was a pullout program, the projects I used with students were meant to supplement what they were already working on in the classroom.

I posted project sheets on the wall 20 at a time. There were four math projects, four science projects, four language arts projects, four social studies projects, and four general projects, which could be applied to any one of the core subjects.

I posted new projects every 6 weeks so that students had fresh choices. I also posted these projects on a website so that if students missed a week of school, they could check the website for reminders and new projects. At the beginning of the year, I showed parents and students the website and gave a short tutorial on how to download projects, calendars, contracts, and logs. This way, everybody—myself, students, and parents—had a clear understanding of what was expected and how it would be accomplished.

Students had complete choice regarding what projects they did. However, if your situation calls for more structure (e.g., if you have very specific learning objectives, if your students need more guidance), then you can easily simply assign projects to students.

All of the learning standards used in these projects are based on the Ohio standards developed by the Ohio Department of Education (2002).

WHAT IF CINDERELLA'S SLIPPERS HAD BEEN GOLD INSTEAD OF GLASS?
■   ■   ■   ■   ■   ■   ■   ■   ■   ■   ■   ■

Brief description: Folktales have been around for hundreds of years, but different cultures have different variations on the same story. For instance, in the Disney version of Cinderella, the heroine has a magical fairy godmother. In the Iraqi version, the godmother takes the form of a red fish, while in the Egyptian version, the godmother is a god. What do these stories indicate about the cultures they come from? You will read an American folktale and compare it to a corresponding version from a foreign country, analyzing what each story's events, characters, and moral(s) indicate about the country it comes from.

Product: You will write an analysis comparing the American version of the story to the foreign one, explaining what the differences in the stories say about the differences in the cultures. You might even want to rewrite the folktale to give it a perspective specific to your state or town.

Content areas: English and Social Studies

Standards:
- English-Reading 5-2
    - o   Identify the influence of setting on the selection.
- Social Studies 2-1
    - o   Describe the cultural practices and products of various groups.

Inspiration starting point: Read the two versions of Cinderella from different cultures.

Estimated time of project: 2 weeks

Suggested materials:
- Books with folktales from a foreign country
- Books on that country's culture

CONSTRUCT A FORT

Brief description: Design and construct the ultimate fort for you and your friends to play in.

Product: For this project, you will have the chance to design the perfect fort, complete with everything you think you might want or need. You will first design the fort on paper, and then you will create a model of the fort. (If you are feeling really ambitious, you may build the fort at home, provided you are supervised by your parents.) You should make sure to include considerations such as area and perimeter. Make sure that your design is structurally sound and mathematically correct before building.

Content area: Math

Standards:

- Math 2-3a
  - o Identify and select appropriate units to measure perimeter.
- Math 2-3a
  - o Identify and select appropriate units to measure area.

Inspiration starting point: Visit http://thetreehouseguide.com to read about and look at photos of the amazing tree houses of the world.

Estimated time of project: 2–3 weeks

Suggested materials:

- Graph paper
- Materials to use for a model, such as popsicle sticks and toothpicks
- Ruler
- Compass

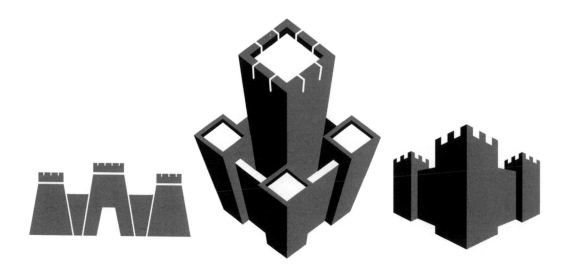

THE THEORY OF FLIGHT

Brief description: The art of making paper airplanes is a complicated one. What makes one plane fly farther than another? What aspects of different designs make one plane better than another?

Product: Here, you will design and construct paper airplanes and fly them to see which of the designs makes the most aerodynamic plane. Through trial and error, you will record the flights of these planes and compare them to those of the other planes. You may determine which design is the most successful, or you may create your own design and test it against the others. Compare and contrast your results with the results in the book (see Inspiration starting point).

Content areas: Science and Math

Standards:
- Science 5-1
    - Select the appropriate tools and procedures to measure and record length.
- Science 6-2
    - Record the results and data from an investigation and make a reasonable explanation.
- Math 5-1
    - Create a plan for collecting data for a specific purpose.

Inspiration starting point: *The Klutz Book of Paper Airplanes* by Doug Stillinger

Estimated time of project: 1–2 weeks

Suggested materials:
- Paper
- Tape measure
- Open area

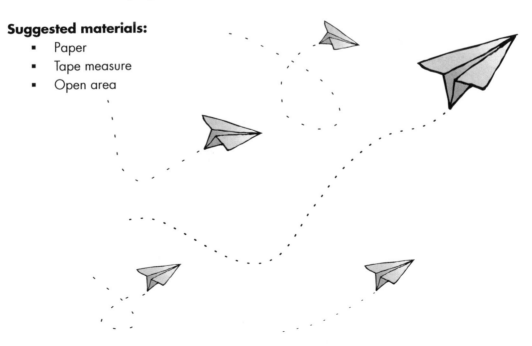

THE LEMONADE STAND

Brief description: Businesses are formed in order to sell products or services to make a profit for the person owning the business. Businesses also provide valuable products or services that some members of the public need or want.

Product: If you were to start your own business, what sort of business would you create, and why? What are some things you could do to ensure success and avoid failure? How would your business compete against other similar businesses? Why would people buy your product or services over those of other businesses?

Content area: Social Studies

Standards:
- Social Studies 4-1
  - Identify the productive resources needed to produce a good or service and suggest opportunity costs for the resources involved.
- Social Studies 4-3
  - Explain how entrepreneurs organize productive resources to produce goods and services and that they seek to make profits by taking risks.

Inspiration starting point: Play Lemonade Tycoon, a simulation game available at http://www.gamehouse.com/download-games/lemonade-tycoon.

Estimated time of project: 2–3 weeks

Suggested materials:
- Local phonebook
- Internet access

I'M JUST A BILL

Brief description: How do certain laws come to be? Why are there different rules for different communities? How did your city's laws become laws? Are any of these laws unfair, or are some laws that should exist missing?

Product: You will look at how the town council functions and what powers it has. This may involve a visit to a council meeting. You could also examine your school rules. Do you think these rules make sense and are fair? How were these laws or rules passed? Most importantly, why do you suppose these laws or rules exist?

Content area: Social Studies

Standard:
- Social Studies 4-4
  - Explain the major responsibilities of the legislative branch.

Inspiration starting point: Watch the Schoolhouse Rock video "I'm Just a Bill."

Estimated time of project: 1–2 weeks

Suggested materials:
- Relevant websites
- A copy of your city's laws or your school's rules

IT'S ALL FUN AND GAMES

Brief description: People use some board games for educational purposes, such as to increase their vocabulary knowledge (Scrabble) or to show off their knowledge of history (Trivial Pursuit).

Product: Here, you will create a board game that is fun to play while at the same time teaching a skill from one of the four core subject areas. Your game should include instructions for how to play and be designed so that people would want to play it.

Content area: Any

Standards: You must choose a single learning standard on which the game will be focused.

Inspiration starting point: Play Scrabble or another educational game on the computer.

Estimated time of project: 2–3 weeks

Suggested materials:
- Materials to create your game board and pieces
- Players to try your new game and offer feedback

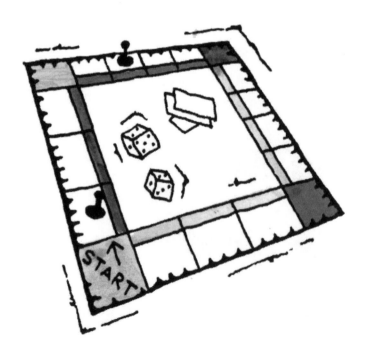

A PICTURE *IS* WORTH A THOUSAND WORDS

■ ■ ■ ■ ■ ■ ■ ■ ■ ■ ■ ■ ■ ■ ■

Brief description: It is often said that a picture is worth a thousand words—in other words, that an image tells the viewer a lot about many different aspects.

Product: Take any piece of artwork, such as Edward Hopper's "Nighthawks" or "Two Sisters" by William-Adolphe Bouguereau and create a short story that tells the story behind the painting. You will have to develop the setting of the story using the clues in the painting and include the people in the painting as characters. Your story should be around 1,000 words and should have a clear plot (beginning, conflict, rising action, resolution).

Content areas: English and Art

Standard:
- Reading and Comprehension 4-11
  - Add descriptive words and details.

Inspiration starting point: Look at William-Adolphe Bouguereau's work "Two Sisters" and imagine where the girls are and what their relationship is like.

Estimated time of project: 2–3 weeks

Suggested Materials
- Piece of art
- Paper and pencil or computer

Two Sisters
by William-Adolphe Bouguereau

YOUR RECOMMENDED READING LIST

■ ■ ■ ■ ■ ■ ■ ■ ■ ■ ■

Brief description: Everyone has an opinion when it comes to books. One person may love a book that others dislike. There are various reasons for this—a book might strike a certain reader in a certain way, or a reader may identify with a certain character or situation in the book, for instance.

Product: Create your own recommended reading list of 10 or more books. For each book, make sure to include the author and title, give a brief summary of why you selected the book, and then explain why you think others should read the book.

Content area: English

Standard:
- Independent Reading 2-9
  - Use criteria to choose independent reading materials.

Inspiration starting point: Look at the recommended reading list for your public library. See if you agree with the library's selections.

Estimated time of project: 2–3 weeks

Suggested materials:
- Library
- Books
- Websites of reading lists

TAKE ME OUT TO THE BALLGAME

Brief description: Baseball is a game involving statistics, percentages, and decimals. This information is figured out in many different ways through various mathematical formulas.

Product: You will follow a specific player or team for a period of time, figuring out things such as batting average, slugging percentage, on-base percentage, and so on. You will track and chart the statistics of the player or team. Then you will analyze this information to determine potential performance for this player or team.

Content area: Math

Standards:
- Number, Number Sense, and Operations 4-7
    - Recognize that division may be used to solve different types of problem situations, and interpret the meaning of remainders.
- Number, Number Sense, and Operations 4-14
    - Demonstrate fluency in adding and subtracting whole numbers and in multiplying and dividing whole numbers by 1- and 2-digit numbers and multiples of 10.

Inspiration starting point: Find books and websites about your favorite players or teams.

Estimated time of project: 3–4 weeks

Suggested materials:
- Newspaper or Internet resources with box scores
- Graph paper or Microsoft Excel

A HERO AIN'T JUST A TYPE OF SANDWICH

Brief description: Spider-Man was created when a radioactive spider bit Peter Parker on the hand. The Fantastic Four got their amazing powers when they were exposed to a cosmic storm in space. The Hulk was exposed to gamma rays that made him turn into a monster every time he got angry. Science has been used in the creation stories of many of the superheroes we have come to enjoy.

Product: You will create a new superhero and draw a comic book chronicling his or her adventures. This superhero must have gained superpowers from a scientific accident. The origin story that you create must explain what scientific principles caused the superhero to gain powers, as well as how those powers work. The superpower demonstrated by your hero must be one of the following:
- the ability to control the wind or other weather patterns;
- the power to cause physical or chemical changes in some way;
- the power to change into different states (i.e., solid, liquid, gas); or
- the power to raise or lower temperature.

Content areas: Science, English, and Art

Standard: You must choose a single learning standard on which the comic book will be focused.

Inspiration starting point: Read Spider-Man or another comic book.

Estimated time of project: 2 weeks

Suggested materials:
- Drawing paper
- Art supplies
- Comic books

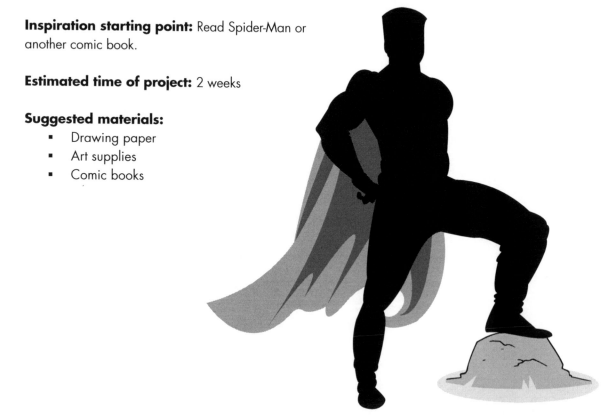

LESSON: TAKING GOOD NOTES

This note-taking lesson, which you could use in a social studies or language arts class, is appropriate for middle school and high school, although you could also modify it for younger students. You will need an overhead or an LCD projector, and it is a longer lecture, so you may wish to break it up.

Students are presented with various methods of taking notes and choose the ones they feel best complement their own learning styles.

Step 1. Distribute Tips on Taking Good Notes and discuss it with students.

Step 2. Describe note-taking methods for students, showing them the included examples (or your own examples based on what your students are currently learning).

- **The outlining method** involves taking notes in an outline format, putting down a main topic in the far-left margin as the top of the outline and indenting related subtopics. When a new topic is introduced, the student goes back to the far-left margin. This way, students can easily tell which information and evidence are associated with which topic.

- **The Cornell method** involves taking notes using columns. The column on the left, where main ideas and terms should go, should be narrower, about 2–3 inches wide. This way, a column of about 6 inches will remain, in which students will write notes about the main ideas and terms. Students should skip a line or two in between main ideas or terms to further separate them. This is an effective method for taking notes on information that will be on a test. The key words and phrases in the left-hand column act as triggers for remembering more detailed information.

- **The mapping method** involves drawing blocks or circles containing main points and important terms, with mapping evidence in connected boxes or circles. This style of note taking is usually attractive to visually oriented students. It does take up a lot of time, which is something that must be taken into account.

Step 3. Once you have introduced the three methods, lecture on a topic your class is learning about—or even show a short educational video—and have the students take some time to practice all of the different methods.

Step 4. You might walk around the room and offer suggestion to students who are missing information, writing down too many facts, and so on.

TIPS ON TAKING GOOD NOTES

Here are some helpful hints on how to write concise notes.

- Don't use complete sentences: Think Tarzan talk.
  - Eliminate articles (e.g., the, a, of).
  - Don't worry about correct punctuation or spelling (except for words you will need to know how to spell).

- Use abbreviations.
  - Native Americans = NA
  - United States = US
  - Because = b/c
  - Environment = Env

- Use symbols.
  - = for definitions
  - / for or
  - + for and

- Use charts.
- Don't assume when it comes to names and dates.
- Combine sentences and information.
- Organization is important. Don't cram all of your notes into a single paragraph. Come up with a system that allows the notes to flow, so that you will be able to find notes easily.
  - Use headings for new aspects or ideas, just as you would make a new paragraph.
  - Outlining is a good way to organize your notes, with numbers, letters, and symbols.

- Don't be too messy, or you won't be able to read your notes later.

EXAMPLE OF THE OUTLINING METHOD OF NOTE TAKING

- The shot heard around the world
  - First battle of the American Revolution
  - British troops attacked Lexington and Concord
    - Wanted to seize weapons at armory
    - The American Minutemen
    - Ready at a moment's notice
  - Took place before America declared Independence

- Old North Bridge
  - Stopped British at Old North Bridge
  - 400 men turned away nearly 100 British troops

- Declaration of Independence
  - Committee of five men wrote it
    - Lists the injustices of King George against colonists
  - Thomas Jefferson credited as main author
  - Ratified July 4, 1776
    - Reason we celebrate Fourth of July

EXAMPLE OF THE CORNELL METHOD OF NOTE TAKING

Shot heard around the world

The first battle of the American Revolution was when English troops advanced on Lexington and Concord in order to seize weapons in the armory there. The American Minutemen, so named because they could be ready at a moment's notice, armed themselves and fired upon the British troops. This took place before America had even declared independence.

Old North Bridge

The Minutemen stopped the British at the Old North Bridge, with about 400 men turning away nearly 100 British troops.

Declaration of Independence

A committee of five men wrote the Declaration of Independence in order to list the injustices that King George had committed against the Colonists. Thomas Jefferson is often credited as the main author of the Declaration. It was ratified on July 4, 1776, which is why we celebrate the Fourth of July.

EXAMPLE OF THE MAPPING METHOD OF NOTE TAKING

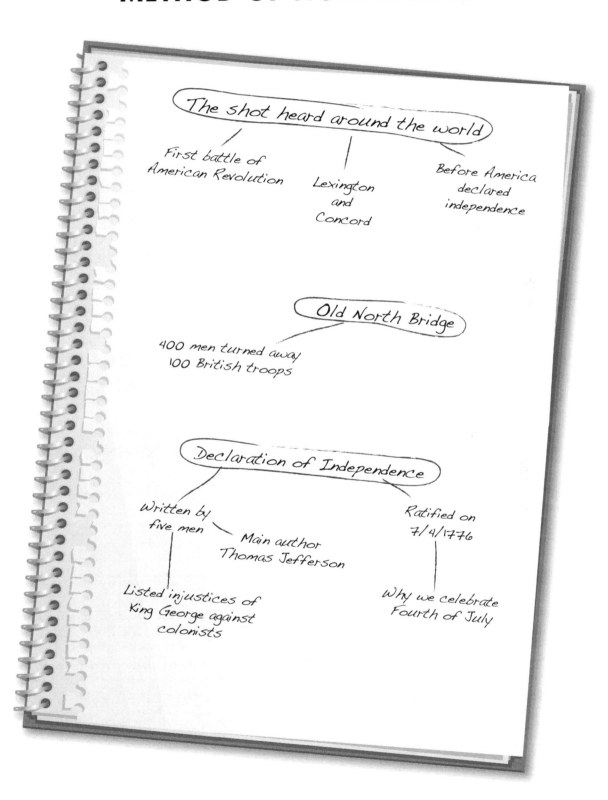

ACTIVITY: COMPASS POINTS

This activity, which takes about an hour, can be used with almost any age level, although you may have to clarify the directions a bit more with younger students. It is an excellent way to foster classroom discussion and help students understand the benefits and challenges of group work.

1. Inform students that they will need to identify themselves as one of the four cardinal directions (points). They may find themselves identifying with a couple of different directions, but they will have to find the single direction that they most identify with, and they cannot select an intermediate direction (e.g., northeast).
2. Read out loud the description of each of the directions. Provide examples to clarify.
3. Once students have identified themselves, assign a direction to each corner of the room and have groups go to their corresponding corners.
4. Have students take 5 minutes to answer the questions on the sheet provided in their groups. Have someone in each group write that group's responses down.
5. Have someone from each group report that group's responses to the rest of the class.
6. Debrief about the activity. What did students learn about how they might work with people from other groups?
7. Discuss the benefits of diversity in groups (e.g., different groups have different strengths, too many of one type of people can cause conflict).

COMPASS POINTS

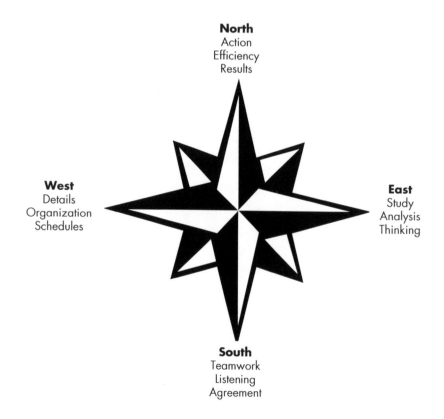

North
Action
Efficiency
Results

West
Details
Organization
Schedules

East
Study
Analysis
Thinking

South
Teamwork
Listening
Agreement

WHAT'S YOUR (COMPASS) POINT?

Group Direction: _____

Group Members: _____

1. Use adjectives to describe some potential **strengths** of your compass point.

    _____

    _____

    _____

    _____

2. Use adjectives to describe some potential **weaknesses** of your compass point.

    _____

    _____

    _____

    _____

3. Which compass point group do you think your group would work best with? Which compass point group do you think would be most challenging for your group to work with?

    _____

    _____

    _____

    _____

4. If a group did not include people of your compass point, how do you think it would function?

    _____

    _____

    _____

    _____

ACTIVITY: PROFILE OF A STUDENT

This activity, which takes about an hour, is more appropriate for older students, although it could be adapted for younger students as well. This activity has been adapted with permission from G. Thompson-Grove (n. d.) with the National School Reform Faculty.

1. Distribute the provided activity sheet to students.
2. Tell students that they must read the descriptions and select the ones that best describe them. Each student will likely identify with numerous descriptions, but each student should pick just one. You can read the descriptions aloud, if you wish.
3. Have students get into groups. You can do this by assigning various numbers to various areas of the room, or you can allow students to discuss their results with classmates—without using numbers—until they believe they are in like-numbered groups. This works better in some cases, because there are so many numbers that some students probably will not have exact matches. If students discuss their results in order to form groups, there is an increased sense of teamwork and personal sharing. In either case, you may have to intervene to help form the groups.
4. Have each group appoint a scribe to record what its members say.
5. Instruct group members to discuss their school experiences.
6. If you wish, instruct groups to allow each group member to speak uninterrupted for 1 or 2 minutes.
7. Instruct students to discuss in their groups what people should know about the group's characteristics if they want to accomplish high-level group work. What should people know about their group? What strategies work best?
8. Have each group report to the rest of the class.
9. Debrief as a class after all of the groups are done reporting. Ask students: What strikes you as you listen to other groups? What does this tell you about how different groups might work together?

WHICH STUDENT ARE YOU?

Student 1. You are life smart, but not school smart. You would do almost anything to avoid looking stupid in school. You are the class clown, or the loud political protester, or the persistent talker—on the verge of being a "behavior problem." You don't mind being sent to the office instead of having to give an oral presentation—and you know just how to get sent there. Everyone at the office knows you well and greets you with affection—they know you as "really, a nice kid." The things you are really good at seem to have little place in school.

Student 2. You are a good student, but you fly under the radar. You have figured out what each of your teachers wants, and you do exactly that—on time, and completely. You are a committed student, but you take few risks, and so you seldom challenge yourself to higher levels of learning. You are the quiet kid whose work always falls within the average range. Because you complete your work, get A's and B's, and are never any trouble, you are often overlooked.

Student 3. You love learning. You can't get enough of it. You actually look up those books that your teachers mention in passing and independently figure out alternative math theorems—just for fun. Your only problem with school is the busy work you have to do and those classes you have to take with kids who just don't seem to care about learning.

Student 4. Who are you, anyway? It often takes teachers a full semester to remember your name, and you often feel invisible. This is either because you like it that way—sitting in the back and hiding behind textbooks, doing decent but unremarkable work to keep a low profile—or because you feel disenfranchised and disempowered. You are sometimes envious of other students, although at other times, you feel above them. You know more about certain subjects than they do, but most teachers don't know that.

Student 5. In your mind, there is no way you can succeed in school. You have been a "remedial" student from before you can remember. You read slowly and seldom get a passing grade on an in-class essay. You do have strengths, but no one seems to notice or value those. You wonder if life in the real world will be like school.

Student 6. You are a finely tuned teacher-pleasing machine. You know exactly what you need to do to maximize your grade, and you do it (no matter what) and then some. You are organized, disciplined, and focused—on your homework, on getting good grades, and on your extracurricular activities, which will look good on your transcript when you apply to college. Your teachers know you will volunteer for anything they ask—and they often do ask.

Student 7. You are as efficient as possible in order to leave time for other things in your life—your mantra is, "The lowest passing grade for the least amount of work." Why pass a class with a 78% when you can pass with a 69.2% and a good sob story? You know all the tricks: make-up tests, rewrites, do-overs, extra credit points, parental pressure, coach pressure, and group work (with the right partners). You put more effort into playing the game than learning.

Student 8. You have a creative mind, you love the arts (drawing, music, drama), and you believe that most of the significant ideas in life can't be expressed by talking or writing, which is all anyone seems to want to do in school. You have a hard time staying focused in most of your required classes. You are happy with yourself, but you often feel like you are marching to the beat of a different drummer.

Student 9. Who says that academics, classes, and grades are the most important things about school? As far as you are concerned, your classes are where you get to see your friends. Frankly, sometimes your work seems to interrupt what's really important—like talking to your friends, going to games, and participating in what they call "extracurricular" activities. These activities don't seem "extra" to you at all—to you, they are central to what school is really about.

BUBBLEGUM PROJECT

I used this project with elementary students, but it could also be adapted to work for middle school. I gave my students 2–3 days to complete this project, which served as an introduction to PBL. The project embraces all of the four core curriculum areas:

- Math
  - o Probability
  - o Percentages
  - o Unit Conversions
- Social Studies
  - o History of gum
  - o Public policy
  - o Public service announcement
- Science
  - o Scientific method
  - o Experiments
  - o Making gum
- English
  - o Analyzing poetry
  - o Writing poetry using the five senses
  - o Creating an ad campaign for gum

MATH

1. Have students estimate the number of gumballs in a full gumball machine.
2. Have students estimate the quantity of each color.
3. According to students' estimations, what percentage of the total number of gumballs does each color represent? The sum of these percentages should equal 100%.
4. Have students count the gumballs to discover the actual overall and per-color quantities. (You could also just tell them!)
5. Students should record the results on a bar graph to represent the data.
6. Have students create two pie charts, one representing the percentages of their estimates, and one representing the actual percentages.
   - o For instance, if the red gumball count is 13%, then the red pie sector should represent 13% of the 360 degrees of a circle ($\approx$ 47 degrees).
   - o Percentage = (number in category ÷ the total) x 100; and 360 x this percentage = degrees of the circle.

7. Have students determine how many gumballs fit . . .
   - o in a foot? (12 inches = 1 foot)
   - o in a mile? (5,280 feet = 1 mile)

SOCIAL STUDIES

1. Students will conduct Internet research on the history of chewing gum and give mini-presentations on what they learned.
   - o   What are the origins of chewing gum?
   - o   How has chewing gum evolved?
   - o   How is chewing gum used today?

2. Next, students will research the gum policy for the school and conduct a debate about whether this policy is fair or unfair.
   - o   Is gum allowed, or not?
   - o   How long has this been the case?

3. After conducting Internet research about gum pollution, students will create public service campaigns to get students to keep the school from having gum all over it.
4. Students will look at different public service announcements and their uses of slogans and images.
5. For homework, students should create posters for their public service campaign.

SCIENCE

1. Tell students they are going to conduct an experiment using the scientific method to determine how long the respective flavors of four types of gum last.* They will be working as a class. A form is provided for them to use to track how long each gum's flavor lasts.
2. Which gum out of the ones students are testing do they think lasts the longest?
3. Students should formulate a hypothesis based on their opinion.
4. Have students make a list of the materials necessary to carry out the experiment. As they are doing this, they should be chewing the first type of gum, noting how long its flavor lasts. (The purpose of this activity is chiefly to reinforce the scientific method, so try to reassure students who are concerned that the validity of the experiment is compromised by them being distracted.)
5. Have students determine what the steps of the procedure should be. List them in chronological order.
6. Have students indicate the experiment's variables, both independent and dependent. (You may have to discuss dependent and independent variables.) At this point, students should move on to the second type of gum. Students could discuss the following questions and how they relate to independent and dependent variables:
   - o   Who is chewing the gum?
   - o   Is the flavor of a previous gum still lingering in the mouth of a participant?
   - o   How much gum has a participant already chewed?
   - o   In what order are the types of gum chewed?
   - o   When do participants record their observations?
   - o   Is 10 minutes enough time to chew each type of gum?

---

*   This is dependent on your school's policy.

    o   Do participants use the same criteria to make observations?

    o   Could the participant mix up gum flavors?

7. Have students indicate what will serve as the control part of the experiment. At this point, students should move on to the third type of gum.

8. Students should create charts and graphs to record their observed results. At this point, they should move to the final type of gum.

9. Have students come to a conclusion.

10. Students can run follow-up experiments in which they see which kinds of gum allow them to blow the largest bubbles.

    o   Each student will determine how the experiment is set up.

    o   Students should report their findings to the class.

11. As an additional follow-up activity, students can create their own chewing gum, experimenting with different flavors, amounts of ingredients, and intensity of taste.

REVIEW: THE SCIENTIFIC METHOD

1. State the problem in the form of a question.
2. State your hypothesis.
3. Make a list of the materials necessary to carry out the experiment.
4. Write down the procedures in detail, listing them in chronological order.
5. Indicate the variables, both independent and dependent.
6. Indicate what will serve as the control part of the experiment.
7. Create charts and graphs to record your observed results.
8. State your conclusion.

HOW LONG DOES THE FLAVOR LAST?

Brand:_____

Flavor:_____

	Very strong	Somewhat strong	Taste still present	Weak	No flavor at all
After 2 minutes					
After 4 minutes					
After 6 minutes					
After 8 minutes					
After 10 minutes					

ENGLISH

1. Students will read the poem "Troublesome Bubble."
   o Students will discuss the poem.
      - How does the poem make them feel?
      - What is the tone of the poem?
      - How does the poem use rhyme?
      - What is the poem's rhyme scheme?
   o Students should discuss the differences between prose and poetry.
      - How could music be considered modern poetry?
      - Is some writing a mixture of poetry and prose?
   o Have the students write poetry or prose about how it feels to chew gum.
      - Use the five senses: touch, sound, sight, taste, and smell.
      - Incorporate details into the written pieces.

2. Students should research and consider the slogans for various brands of gum.
   o Juicy Fruit:_____
   o Doublemint: _____
   o Extra:_____
   o Winterfresh: _____
   o Big Red:_____
   o Orbit:_____
   o Freedent: _____
   o Big League Chew:_____
   o Bubble Tape: _____

3. Discuss with students how the slogans make them feel, and which audiences specific gums seem to be targeting.
4. Discuss the marketing strategies of familiar products with students.
5. Discuss various methods that marketers use to sell gum and how these methods depend on their audiences (e.g., Bazooka Gum became popular after including cartoons in its packaging).
6. Students should create a hypothetical gum and figure out how to market it, using strategies such as:
   o fancy packaging,
   o unique flavors,
   o product tie-ins, and
   o creative improvements such as flavor boosters.

7. Students should identify the audience for their product and figure out how they will effectively sell their product to that audience.
8. Have students create an advertising campaign including a slogan, a package design, and a commercial to sell the gum.

Troublesome Bubble
By Todd Stanley

I was sitting in math class one cold rainy day,
Dreaming my terrible boredom away,
When I reached in my pocket and then—ah!—I found
A tiny round object, wrapped up and bound.

I took this thing out and I saw in plain view
Here was a morsel I simply must chew!
A nice piece of gum I'd forgotten about—
I unwrapped it slowly and kept a lookout.

I had to be careful; I couldn't be seen—
Frankly, I really was not very keen
To be caught by our teacher, who'd made it quite clear
Being caught chewing gum should fill students with fear!

One boy was caught with some gum just last week,
And now he is gone—not one word, not one peep!
We don't know where to, we do not have a hunch—
But one rumor says he's been turned into lunch!

Chewing this trifle, I risked life and limb,
But life without gum would be ever so dim!
The gorgeous aroma was too much to take,
Like sweet-smelling cookies your mother might make.

I slipped the gum quietly right past my lip
Like a cool drink of water—I took a small sip,
And then I bit down on that sugary pill—
Chewing, I tried very hard to keep still.

But it tasted so good I got carried away
And started to chomp like a cow eating hay!
I knew I'd be caught; I was ready to sing—
But Teacher was too busy with teacher things.

And then all too fast, my gum ran out of taste!
All my fine chewing had been a big waste.
There was one thing to do with my chewed-up confection
(If Teach would just look in the other direction).

With my tongue to my teeth, then, I started to push
On the soft wad of blubber I'd chewed to a mush.
It grew bigger and bigger—before I could stop,
It got out of control and gave quite a loud pop!

Teach halted the lesson and walked to my side—
I had to be wise, now, I couldn't be snide—
But when Teacher asked what all the noise was about,
I turned to respond and I left not a doubt.

Across my whole nose there was rubbery slop—
To clean it, I'd probably need a strong mop!
I'd fallen for gum; I had taken the bait—
That troublesome bubble had just sealed my fate.

About the Author

Todd Stanley, a National Board Certified Teacher, has been in the classroom for the past 14 years in a myriad of positions. He spent the early years of his career compacting gifted curriculum in a junior high program called Horizons. He went on to work as a facilitator at the Christopher Program, a project-based, interdisciplinary program for juniors and seniors from around central Ohio. He then created the Ivy Program, a gifted pull-out program for third and fourth graders. He also traveled around Ohio presenting on the Literacy Curriculum Alignment Program, training school staff members how to write short-cycle assessments, align their curriculum, and enrich students' learning experiences.

For the past 4 years, he has been teaching project-based learning to fifth- and sixth-grade gifted students and will open a new program next year involving fifth to eighth graders that includes vertical articulation, inquiry-based learning, and of course, project-based learning. He has taught at summer camps for gifted students, spending several years at the Summer Institute for the Gifted before moving on to his current position with the Ohio Wesleyan University Junior League. He received his master's degree from The Ohio State University. He lives in Pickerington, OH, with his wife, Nicki, and two daughters, Anna and Abby.